5

POSTERS OF PROTEST AND REVOLUTION

POSTERS OF PROTEST AND REVOLUTION

Selected and reviewed by Maurice Rickards

ADAMS & DART

0239 000250

First published in 1970 by Adams & Dart
40 Gay Street, Bath, Somerset
All rights reserved
Designed by Maurice Rickards, MSIA
Text printed letterpress by Billing & Sons Limited, Guildford and London
Illustrations printed offset by Alfieri & Lacroix, Milan
Bound in England

On the morning of 31 October 1517 the Professor of Biblical Literature at Wittenberg University took a hammer and nails and fixed a large piece of paper to the door of Wittenberg Castle church.

The professor's name was Luther. On the paper were written his ninety-five points of dissent from the teachings of the Church. His action was the prelude to a chain of events that was to rock the sixteenth century. It was to prove not merely an isolated act of defiance; it was the first step in the founding of a new Church, a denomination whose adherents were ultimately to number millions.

Martin Luther broke new ground in religion, but he also broke new ground in an incidental matter: he was among the first ever to devise and display a Poster of Protest and Revolution.

To minds attuned to the forms of twentieth-century protest, the whole pattern of Luther's career has a familiar look. There was public demonstration, deliberate and unambiguous; there was disputation, commotion and ferment; there was the summons to appear at the bar of authority— a confrontation with force of numbers: 'Luther was ushered into the august presence', says one report: 'The assembly was the most magnificent that Europe could furnish. Two hundred and four judges were there; the emperor, six electors, eighty dukes, eight margraves, thirty prelates, seven ambassadors, and hosts of princes and deputies.' Authority was taking no chances.

Luther faced them alone: 'pale and emaciated, he stood before them. . . .' There were the familiar expressions of official apprehension; steps had to be taken, Authority said, 'to check the growth of new and dangerous opinions'. Finally, naming him as a 'fiend in human form', they issued a writ against him, banning him.

There were official book-burnings; in Rome, Cologne and Louvain there were bonfires of Luther's writings. In reply, in the now well-established convention of draft-card destruction, there were popular burnings of official documents. Often these were combined with processions of protest: 'At nine in the morning he led a band of professors, doctors and students to the gate of the city, and threw into the bonfire, kindled for the purpose, the canon law, the decretals, the Clementines and the Extravagantes of the popes, tossing after them into the flames the papal bull. . . .'

There was also, as in more recent times, the final act of defiance, the point of no return. On 11 June 1512 Martin Luther, priest of Wittenberg, married Katherina von Bora—herself lately from a nunnery.

And at the beginning of it all there was the poster.

By present definition, the Wittenberg exhibit only just qualifies as a poster. The twentieth-century connoisseur lays down clear-cut rules as to what is, and what is not, a poster. For admission into the official listings the true poster must fulfil four distinct conditions.

Firstly, says the connoisseur, the poster must be a separate sheet, *affixed* to an existing surface (as opposed to those markings and images rendered directly on the surface). Secondly, it must embody a *message*; a mere decorative image is not enough. Thirdly, it must be *publicly displayed*. Finally, it must have been *multipally produced*; a single hand-done notice is not a poster within the meaning of the act.

Printing in Luther's time was still largely in the hands of its inventors. His poster was decidedly a single hand-done item. It relied for its reproduction on the dedication of copyists. In hundreds of hand-done versions it appeared, either as a public notice or as a 'leaflet', in every major town in Europe. But if its claim to posterdom is weak, the Luther document's role as an instrument of protest and revolution is unquestioned. It is in direct line of succession from the wall-graffiti from which the connoisseurs distinguish it; it was on paper—and it was noticeably longer in wordage.

The Wittenberg poster has not survived; we cannot reproduce it in the present collection. But we do know that in the matter of length it was uncharacteristic, either of the graffiti that preceded it or of the orthodox poster of today. It bore ninety-five items—some 2,500 words.

This, for any poster, is a lot of words. That they claimed as much attention as they did is a testimony not only to the fact that they were important words, but also to the comparative lack of competition.

Prior to Luther, as well as in recent times, protesters set much store on brevity. The time factor, in writing the message as well as in reading it, is crucial. For the slogan-dauber there is not only the obvious danger of a long message being ignored but the additional danger of being interrupted in mid-slogan. For the latter-day protester—whether direct-on-walls or on-a-separate-sheet-affixed—the competition hazard is immeasurably increased. Whatever the medium, the sloganeer prefers the monosyllable, the compound and the four-letter word.

In the twentieth century the slogan has become almost an art-form in itself; it has developed its own refinements, its own disciplines and its own connoisseurs. Some enthusiasts, dissatisfied with the efforts of the professionals, have even taken to the devising of graffiti for their own sake. (Among these it may be recorded that towards the end of the 'sixties a notable invention was *Keep the Pope off the moon.*)

But for the serious protester, slogans are real and earnest. Above all, they are brief. It must be said, though, that brevity has its disadvantages; as it runs away with itself it relies more and more on the background knowledge of the reader. Taken out of context, or at a distance of time and place, the brevities of *A bas l'art. 47!* or *Nein, niemahls!* are brief to the point of extinction. In Ghent in 1886 or the Saargebiet in 1935 they were relevant; to the distant view they are meaningless.

More meaningful—because better publicised—are the brevities of *Yanks go home* and *Rusové domu* (Czech for *Russians go home*). Equally short, in a language not noted for its conciseness, is the Italian *W il Re*; with their contraction of *W* for *Viva* the Italians have a distinct advantage: there are few languages in which it is possible to render *Long live the King* in only five characters. In similar vein, and with equally high compression, the Irish have *Up Dev* (Irish for *Viva De Valera*).

In some parts of the world the use of initials alone (*FWA* for *Free Wales Army*) compresses things still further. But *FWA* is merely declamatory. In August 1968 the Czechs brought an added twist to the use of initials by the manner of their rendering; in a reference to the German occupation of World War II they wrote up the letters U *SS* R.

If it is the function of the slogan to present a maximum of meaning in a minimum of compass, there is clearly a place for the irreducible minimum—the symbol. Here we move fully into the field of the ideogram, if not of the secret sign. The Campaign for Nuclear Disarmament has its semaphores, *N* and *D* superimposed. The early Christians had an outline of a fish. This, the secret sign of an underground organisation, conveyed a forbidden proposition: the Greek word for fish—*ichthus*—combines the initial letters of the expression *Iesus Christos Theos Huios Sotia*—Jesus Christ, Son of God, Saviour.

Whatever its merits, encapsulation has its disadvantages. The use of initials or the single symbol gives most value for least effort, but it also suffers from a lack of human interest. For the greatest impact, say the connoisseurs, the wall inscription should evoke the ordinary forms of familiar speech; ideally there should be a verb—if only a subjunctive—and it should convey in the manner of its execution the urgency and feeling of the moment. In short, says the connoisseur, impact must be emotional rather than intellectual.

In the early days of graffiti and the one-off official notice, there was a compromise between brevity and impact. Then, as in the twentieth century, wordiness was exceptional. But in the evolutionary period, when printing was still getting into its stride, there was a swing in the opposite direction. To make the most of the new medium, and to impress the rank and file, Authority let itself go. There came the era of the printed Proclamation or Broadsheet.

In the discursive manner of the Peace Treaty or Diktat, the public notice blossomed into Section, Sub-section and Paragraph. It ran to as many words as possible. Often it bore a crest as heading and started with the words *Whereas* or *By Virtue of the Powers vested in Me*. . . . Always it bore an 'official' look; often it contrived to look threatening. Sometimes it finished with a signature and a date; mostly there was a suggestion of a seal.

The Proclamation Style became an accepted convention. It was the printed counterpart of the speech from the throne, complete with fanfare of trumpets. It was the voice of Authority multiplied; with careful planning it could be released simultaneously over a wide area. It was an instrument of government, and it worked.

It is not surprising that, when the occasion arose for people to answer back, they did so in the same idiom. In their earliest forms, posters of protest and revolution were merely proclamations—counter-proclamations, as we may call them. Adopting the same techniques of presentation, the same official look and the same tendency to flowery language, they spoke back in the voice of authority.

Not only protesters, but politicians and pill-pedlars followed suit. So general did this mimicry eventually become, the French Government was obliged in self-defence to pass a law forbidding the use of white paper except for Government declarations. It was this law that was to give the streets of nineteenth-century France their characteristic look of multicoloured chaos. It is still in force today.

Devoid of illustration, the Proclamation Style has an impact all its own. It has a long and eventful history; it remains in the twentieth century as effective as it ever was. For announcing mobilisation, for imposing curfews, for reporting outrages and the shooting of hostages, for incitement to disaffection and non-cooperation—it has a hundred uses. It stretches back through history as a handy all-purpose instrument of persuasion. Even in days of radio and television, where direct speech might be thought to have come into its own, it still appears as a final seal of confirmation 'in writing'.

Its air of respectability gives it great advantage; in Scotland in 1572 under the heading *Proclamatioun* there appeared a 500-word poster; it was posted throughout the country and it had the unmistakable 'official' look. It was entitled *Ane Advertissement to the Faithful, that Euery Ane may understand the Bludie and Tressonable Interprises of the Papists*. It was published by James Douglas, Earl of Morton, and it gave a detailed report—bogus from start to finish—of the schemings of the Pope and his Catholic princes in a secret league to extirpate Protestants.

On 16 August 1914, in similar style, the German Emperor announced his departure from the capital. The calls of war, he said, obliged him to take leave of his Headquarters in Berlin. 'I trust in God,' he said, 'and in the valour of our Army and Navy and in the indomitable spirit of unity of the German people in their hour of danger. . . .' In its presentation, in its sense of occasion and sovereign dignity, and above all with its gothic imperial *Wilhelm I R*, it had the air of a major victory.

As an instrument of mobilisation, too, the printed Proclamation has served well. Its authority has been unanswerable. Even as a device for voluntary recruitment it has brought results. In 1770 the Corps Royal of the Artillerie de France announced its manpower needs (*de par le Roi*) saying—with only the briefest lapse into advertising-ese—that *les Jeunes Gens qui désirent entrer au Service de Sa Majesté ne peuvent choisir un Corps plus avantageux. . . . La Paie plus forte que dans aucune autre Troupe, augmente jusqu'à vingt-un sols par jour. . . .*

King George V of England, himself no stranger to the power of proclamation, in 1916 signed a document under the royal crest and datelined *Buckingham Palace.* It appeared on hoardings all over the country as a poster/proclamation. Headed *To my People,* it began, *At this grave moment in the struggle,* and went on to call for men to come forward voluntarily and take their places in the fight. *More men and yet more are wanted to keep my armies in the field. . . .* The poster served, in the last months before the introduction of conscription, to add another few hundred thousand men to those who had already died.

When conscription in Britain finally came it was heralded, inevitably, by a Proclamation. This, with its accustomed air of finality, was for most of the population beyond challenge. But there were some areas where it was less so.

In one or two of the bigger cities of Ireland there appeared a rejoinder— one of the few recorded examples of a specific poster-reply to a specific poster-announcement. This [32] with its ringing phrases and its rallying call, is a classic example of the counter-proclamation. It was small, but it was numerous; some 5000 copies of it mysteriously appeared on the walls and lamp-posts of Dublin one morning. Its presence was widely noted (not least by the Irish billposters, who scented the danger not only of insurrection but of non-Federation competition). Though it lacked crest, date and signature, for the many thousands who saw it the poster was the voice of authority.

The Irish were familiar with the counter-proclamation. For long periods it was the only articulate voice of opposition. Over the years it had become a recognised vehicle for polemic and rhetoric; the clarion calls of the counter-proclamationists grew louder and longer. In bold face, italics and underlinings, with exclamation marks often doubled and trebled, they thundered from barn-door, wall and tree. 'And if the country should produce anyone mean and traitorous enough not to obey this appeal,' said one proclaimant, reaching the climax of a call to anti-landlord action, 'let him be marked out as one with whom no person should hold friendly social relations. No-one should buy from him or sell to him. No-one should speak to him. Let him be shunned as if he were covered with some horrible loathsome disease. . . .' When time and money permitted, the Irish counter-proclamation was never short of dramatics or colourful writing.

* *Numbers in brackets refer to illustrations.*

At the first real crunch, in the Easter week of 1916, there appeared the proclamation of the 'Provisional Government of the Irish Republic' [98]. This, printed the day before the taking of the Dublin GPO, was read aloud by its author, Padraic Pearse, from the steps of the building. Here, on a less hysterical note, but not without its conscious sense of occasion, is the real-and-earnest language of protest and revolution: 'In the name of God, and of the dead generations from which she receives her old tradition of nationhood, Ireland, through us, summons her children to her flag and strikes for her freedom. . . .'

The insurgents numbered 1500; the British forces were about 20,000. Fighting was fierce; with fires raging throughout Dublin's centre area, with the Post Office building almost destroyed by British shelling and incendiary bombs, with James Connolly wounded and directing the insurgents from a stretcher, there was just one more proclamation [100] before the end. Within seven days the rising was quelled. A fortnight later all of the signatories of the proclamation had been executed. It was to be another 33 years and a lot more shooting later, before Pearse's 'sovereign independent state' was to begin to emerge.

From whichever side of the political or military fence the Pearse manifestoes are viewed, their central core of courage and conviction is inescapable. Classically, posters of protest and revolution fall broadly into two categories: they are either typographic—the most that can be managed within the budget and in the heat of the moment, or pictorial—the more polished and leisurely product of a long-drawn action. It is in the category of the typographics that the heat of the moment is often most poignantly apparent. In the Irish proclamations, perhaps above all others, it comes through unmistakably.

More particularly in their inadequacies, in their makeshift type-setting and occasional misprints, posters of protest convey their urgency. On a thousand hurried occasions, sometimes under stress, sometimes even under fire, printing has been fumbled, with letters transposed or omitted, under- or over-inking of the impression, and uneven make-ready.

Biggest hazard of all—perhaps intrinsic to the revolutionary situation—is the last-minute change of policy, the behind-the-scenes battle within the high command. Though their details remain for ever a matter of secret history, they may still leave traces of their passing. *Order No. 1* of the Petrograd Soviet of Workers' and Soldiers' Deputies [142] offers scope for conjecture. We may infer from the empty space that separates the last paragraphs that something has been deleted. (An item No. 8, perhaps?) All that remains is a speckle of battered type to mark the spot.

Sometimes a difficulty is shortage of type—particularly where the same announcement may have to be set up and printed secretly in a number of different localities at once. Mindful of the hazard, the Munich Executive of the Workers' and Soldiers' Soviets in 1919 took steps to avoid it. When they put out their General Strike poster [81] they first made a block of it.

As the marking between the lines in the illustration shows, the announcement was first set up in type and then reproduced in the form of an all-over printing plate. A number of stereotypes taken from the original were then distributed to chosen printers, allowing the same announcement, identical in every detail, to be printed and distributed simultaneously. The irregular markings show the edges of the printed stereotype; in the hurry to get the proclamation through the machines there has been excessive pressure of the paper on the printing surface. This has caused it to print the image of the lower level of the plate as well as of the raised letters.

(It may also be noted that, for all the efficiency of the Executive's print production planning, the final line excluding restaurants from the strike has the air of an addendum. Was this an Executive afterthought?)

The technical hitch is a hazard at the best of times; in emergency it looms larger; the stress of the moment may produce the most elementary of technical errors. A typical example (not in this case a proclamation but a do-it-yourself stencil-cut) is the Sorbonne student's *ORTF* poster [188]. This design, one of a large number produced at the height of the 1968 disturbances, appeared in two editions. In one of them the lettering was the wrong way round, in the other the right way round. It seems clear that in the excitement of the moment the artist who cut the image for the first edition made a fundamental mistake; he rendered the lettering on the screen the right way round, forgetting that in printing on to paper the image would be reversed.

Sometimes the wording itself shows signs of hurry. In a proclamation of 7 November 1918 [78], the Munich Workers' and Soldiers' Soviet ordered Post and Telegraph personnel back to their jobs. It seems to have been from force of habit that in doing so the Revolutionary Council still referred to them as members of the *Royal* Post and Telegraph Offices. The word comes oddly from a Workers' and Soldiers' Soviet.

(We may notice in the matter of wording that a proclamation published a few months later [85] makes an inverted concession to a time-honoured tradition: as a substitute for the phrase 'by virtue of the powers vested in me' it says, 'according to ordinances concerning the state of siege and to be published later'.)

The proclamation has been used not only as a straightforward announcement. It has also been used as a straightforward purveyor of untruth (as with the *bludie and tressonable interprises* announcement of 1572) and it has been used as a weapon against its alleged authors. In the American Civil War, the Southerners published a proclamation quoting a disreputable order [130] allegedly issued from the New Orleans headquarters of the United States army. The device, whether genuine or false, is a standard gambit. In Edinburgh in the 1820s there appeared a poster purporting to announce a strike of maid-servants. This, at first glance a genuine protest against bad pay and working conditions, proves on closer reading to have been concocted by a critic to poke fun at the movement for working-class militancy. Among the 'demands' in the proclamation is entitlement to automatic acquisition of mistresses' old clothes.

The pictorial poster came into its own in the last decades of the nineteenth century. By the early 1900s it was an accepted idiom of communication. It had evolved its own visual grammar, its own production and distribution channels and its role in the social scene.

As a medium of persuasion—commercial, social or political—it superseded both the newspaper and the broadsheet. Its development, a direct result of Senefelder's discovery of the lithographic principle half a century before, allowed full-scale mass production of the visual image. Where previously there had been reliance on the relatively primitive woodcut, lithography opened the way to refinements of graphic treatment. The crude flat areas of the poster woodcut gave way to subtleties of tone and colour never before attained in quantity. The era of the multiple image had begun.

By the outbreak of the 1914 war the technique had reached high standards of production efficiency. In some areas it had also acquired the status of a parenthetic art form. In France it had gained complete acceptance. Toulouse-Lautrec, Bonnard, Steinlen and a number of other artists had brought it to a full flowering, not only on the public hoardings, but in the private collections and galleries of the connoisseur.

In 1914 the medium was mobilised for war. In 1918 in Russia it was mobilised for revolution. In the history of posters of dissent its appearance there marks a dividing line between the era of the broadsheet and that of the poster as we have come to know it.

The pictorial poster, with its marked advantage over the broadsheet in colour and attractiveness, had everywhere the advantage of the image over the letter. In Europe at large, levels of literacy were low. In Russia at the turn of the century some seventy-five per cent. of the population was illiterate. The picture-poster was not merely an adjunct to persuasion—it was a centre-point. The Revolution took its posters seriously.

1914 had signed up its Hassalls and Hohlweins, its Forains and James Montgomery Flaggs; 1918 in Russia recruited its own artists. Of these, Dmitri Stakheyevitch Orlov (D. S. Moor by signature), Lizitsky and Rodchenko are perhaps best known; there were dozens of others. As with the 1914-18 war posters the designs were infused not only with the artistic integrity of their authors, they had the added impact of personal conviction. In the ordinary commercial field the artist may bring to his work a moderate warmth (Steinlen had lent charm to Nestlé's Milk, and Toulouse-Lautrec had not been above a design for bicycle chains); but when it comes to the poster of conviction—protest, war or revolution—he brings heat. The work of Moor and his contemporaries in Russia is typical.

These posters, imbued at once with an idealistic drive and a ringing call to action, were remarkable not only for their sense of conviction but for their immediacy. Earlier, revolutionaries had hurriedly set up type for the 'counter-proclamation' poster; here, in Kiev, Vitebsk, Petrograd, Moscow and a score of other cities, full-blown colour posters came off the litho presses even as battles were fought.

Petrov's posters for the defence of Petrograd and the Urals [49, 51] were produced as Kolchak's armies attacked in the east, and Yudenich threatened in the west. Kolchack had established a counter-revolutionary government. Foreign troops had been landed in various parts of the country. British and French contingents moved in at Vladivostok, followed soon by Japanese and Americans. The French were in Odessa and much of the territory of western Siberia was occupied by Czechs. Over the whole country there was a chaos of armies, uprisings, actions and counter-actions. The Allies, preoccupied with their struggle with Germany, found time and resources to help the White armies. Generals Kolchak, Denikin and Yudenich—and later Wrangel—were supplied by Allied governments. The tanks that Yudenich used against the Red Army in the drive towards Petrograd were British.

Denikin got to within 200 miles of Moscow. Yudenich was only ten miles from Petrograd. But by the spring of 1920 the whole of the counter-revolutionary action had collapsed.

The posters reflect the military pressures and urgencies of the period. They also take time out for social exhortation. *Wrangel is still alive; Finish him off without mercy!* said a poster by Moor in July 1920. But, said another, unsigned, in four different language editions—Russian, Polish, Yiddish and Tartar—*Education is the road for Communism.* In another poster Moor demands of the Cossacks, erstwhile supporters of the Tsar and the old régime: *Whose side are you on—theirs or ours?* [147]. A poster by Radakhov [63] points to the perils of illiteracy: *The illiterate is a blind man; failure and disaster await him.* It is a bizarre pattern—a layer-cake of pugnacity and social conscience.

In the years that followed, as the régime began to settle down, the stress was increasingly on the social side, on education, on health and hygiene and on help for the needy. In 1921, in the Ukraine and in the regions of the North Caucasus and the Volga, there was a complete failure of the grain crop. In the famine that followed, over 1,000,000 peasants took refuge in makeshift camps near rivers and railways and on the outskirts of the big towns. It was estimated that some 20-30 million people were affected by the failure—a calamity as great as that of the Tsar's famine of 1891. The posters by Moor, *Help!* [39], and Simakov, *Remember the hungry* [40], are graphic reminders of the scale of the disaster.

The *Help!* design, with its tragic figure and stark background, is one of the most powerful 'appeal' posters ever published. Many of the posters put out by the revolutionary government have now, not surprisingly, a dated look; this one has not. It is of special interest that it conveys its message with a single word and a single image in a single printing—black.

The campaign directed to women in the Soviet Union has been a continuing operation. Even as recently as the 1930s Soviet posters were exhorting women to take their productive place in an industrial society. In the early 1920s the going was more difficult; in a double-barrelled appeal to the worker, a 1923 poster [12] urges the end of prostitution and the acceptance of women as workers in the factories; *In destroying capitalism the proletariat will also destroy prostitution; prostitution is the great evil of humanity; workers respect honour and the woman worker!*

(It may be noticed that this poster, which is unsigned, has an unusually cluttered and crowded appearance. Unlike its contemporaries, which aim at a clear-cut simplicity, the design shows signs of 'design by committee'. Not only is it visually clumsy, but in the combining of two distinct issues in one message it is open to the risk of irreverent interpretation. The design is further complicated by the disparity in the size of the two principal figures. The observer may wonder why the woman is shown as a midget. And as a final perplexity, with the man well-shod, why should she be shoe-less?)

For the most part the Russian revolutionary poster is unambiguous. Often it has a simplicity and economy of image that put it years ahead of its time. Lizitsky's famous 'wedge' poster [52] although its symbolism is unmistakable, carries simplicity to a point perhaps beyond acceptance by the man on the factory floor. The 1920s saw much that was radically new to the Russian eye. In a sweeping away of the old images there was a headlong drive to novelty—to 'destructivism', 'constructivism', 'cubism', 'suprematism', and a whole series of revolutionary *arts nouveaux*—each in turn condemned as bearing hidden traces of the old régime.

In posters there were traces of the past not only in style and treatment, but sometimes even in content. Ivanov's design for the celebration of May 1 [92], with its flower-scattering angel-figure, shows little sign of -isms of any sort. And in a poster celebrating the third anniversary of the

Revolution [64] the ancient image of St George and the Dragon is invoked—here in proletarian role. (It may be noted that St George has appeared for a number of defendants in the calendar of the poster. In World War I he did poster duty for the Austrians and the British simultaneously.)*

The old images were a long time dying in Russia. Some of them were so deeply rooted, and the changes so confusing, that peasants at funerals were reported to have carried the red flags of the Workers' Councils and miracle-working ikons in the same procession. In remote areas country women dedicated candles and had masses said for the repose of the soul of the deceased Lenin. It is not surprising if, in some of their posters, the revolutionaries mixed their metaphors.

Lizitsky, in the opinion of many, was too far ahead of himself altogether. He, and the rest of the avant-garde, were soon eclipsed by the coming of Socialist Realism—the down-to-earth no-nonsense representationalism of the ordinary man. This, an idiom which is itself a long time dying, eschews the conceits of symbolism and calls a revolutionary spade a spade. Although virtually abandoned in other areas (Cuba, for example, and Spain in the 1930s) it has re-emerged, freshly painted but clearly recognisable, in the China of the 'sixties and 'seventies.

Straddled as it was between the past and the future, Russia in the 1920s was quick to move into the world of the new technologies. Typical of its readiness to embrace new ideas was the introduction, many years before its adoption by the rest of the world, of the propaganda train. These, with coaches painted along their whole length with propaganda pictures and messages, constituted mobile posters of truly spectacular scale. It cannot be said that these wide-screen designs contributed much to the sum total of graphic achievement, but their impact over vast stretches of the Russian countryside was enormous. The outside of the carriages carried suitably attenuated scenes—Lenin sweeping away the litter and debris of the capitalist past, Red Army cavalry charges, workers' processions and the like—captioned with similarly extended slogan strips. Inside, the carriages provided walk-through exhibition areas, teaching aids and literacy campaign material.

But it was on the poster, till then almost exclusively the instrument of a bourgeois society, that the message of the revolution largely relied.

Across the battlefront, in Germany, there were posters too. As war morale crumbled the threat of trouble grew. So strong were the signs of discontent, there were many among the Russians who believed that a call for a German general strike would be enough to end the war. As it turned out it was a close-run thing. In Bavaria, insurrectionary broadsheets and posters broke out in a rash. Elsewhere, government posters called in turn for calm, for men to protect the hearth and home from the Red Terror,

* *'Posters of the First World War'*, Evelyn, Adams & Mackay, Nos. 64, 65.

for the suppression of anarchy, for a hero's welcome for the returning men of the forces, for a rallying round the Fatherland, and for fair shares of food for town and country.   On all hands the poster clamoured.

In the pre-war years the German poster had been thin on the hoardings. A police censorship, arbitrary and inconsistent, had discouraged enterprise.   One poster, a Käthe Kollwitz design put out by the Greater Berlin Propaganda Council, showed ragged children, victims of overcrowded slums and squalor: *600,000 Berliners live three—and more—to a room; hundreds of thousands of children have no play space.*   The police condemned the poster as 'offensive'.   It was withdrawn.   In 1914 a poster by Karl Stadler advocating votes for women [15] came under fire.   The poster, put out as part of Red Week, and clearly 'left' in tenor, was described by the Berlin police as 'offensive to the authorities'.   It did not appear in Berlin.

The Prussian Press Act gave to the local chief of police a virtually free hand.   Article 9 of the Act forbade posters altogether—with the exception of 'announcements of meetings which are not themselves banned by law; of public entertainments; of articles lost, stolen or found, and of sales information'.   The field for the non-commercial poster—certainly for the poster of dissent—was limited.   But in the war years the rules were waived; the hoardings shouted exhortation.   In the period of the *debâcle* there was more to come.

On 3 November 1918 the German Grand Fleet mutinied at Kiel.   Five days later Bavaria declared a Workers' Republic.   In Berlin a Council of People's Delegates assumed power.   On 20 November a Conference of Workers and Soldiers Delegates was demanding nationalisation of German industries.   Day by day, almost hour by hour, the uncensored walls of Munich carried the story of the rising.

At 10.30 on the morning of 7 November von Brettreich, Statesminister Royal for the Interior, put out a broadsheet appealing to everyone to do his duty and maintain calm and order.   That same evening the Workers' and Soldiers' Council put out their own broadsheet.   It announced that the Proletariat had thrown off its shackles and 'joyfully freed itself'; it enjoined members of the public, under the protection of the revolutionaries, to maintain calm and order.   'Long live peace,' it concluded, 'down with the dynasty!'   (It was here, in an instruction published simultaneously, that the revolutionaries required the personnel of the Royal Post and Telegraph Office to do their duty.)

In the revolutionary situation, 'law and order' serves as a classic chopping-block.   On the one hand, the Establishment avows its concern for the preservation of law and order; on the other the revolutionary seeks, once it is disrupted, to restore it.   In blast and counterblast from both sides, each offers the ordinary man the same desirable prize.   The words 'law and order' run through the proclamations of the Bavarian revolution as a *leitmotiv.*

The revolution lasted six months.   The last of its many proclamations announced that Government troops had surrounded Munich.   '*Listen to the voice of reason!   Clear the streets and squares. . . .*'   On 30 April it was all over.   But the law and order that followed was ill at ease; everywhere in Germany there was still the threat from within, still the Red Terror that blazed in the East.   Posters still called their warnings.

The poster crop for 1919 was for the most part typographic, but there were a few pictorial issues.   These were put out by the Establishment— either officially or through private organisations.   They fell for the most part into four categories, all in varying degrees of support of law and order.

There was the welcome-home-hero appeal [103], devised as a stabilising influence on returning soldiery; there was the explicit condemnation of anarchy (Suchodolski's bomb-rejecting family man [10] is typical); there was the Red Terror Scare poster [19, 24, 27, 28, 29]; and finally there was the direct appeal [76, 82] to the homecoming soldier to join up with one of the near-illegal Freiheitskorps—local training detachments devised as a way round the 100,000-man limit imposed by Versailles.

War, said Clausewitz, is politics continued by other means.   Revolution stands in a similar relationship to protest.   In Germany in the post-war years revolution simmered.   So did war.   Against both—and in aid of both, there was protest.   There was protest against war; Käthe Kollwitz in 1924 said simply *NO MORE WAR* [7]; in 1928, as the German government laid plans for the building of a number of battle cruisers, the Socialist Party called for a plebiscite [5].   Said their poster, *Sign against Battlecruisers and War!*

In 1921 a plebiscite over the future of Upper Silesia produced a state bordering on open insurrection.   It brought bilingual protests [109, 110] and German-language anti-German posters [108, 111] from the Polish faction. Passive resistance to the French occupying forces in the Ruhr in 1923 brought the poster *No, I will not be intimidated!* [107].   It also brought France and Germany to the brink of a new war.   Soon it was to lead to the fall of the Mark.   Inflation, by November 1923, had raised the price of a single newspaper to two hundred thousand million marks.

Election posters sketch the story of the years that followed.   In 1932 the German workless figure was 5,800,000.   In the winter of 1932 it topped 6,000,000.   That was the winter in which Hans Schweitzer's well-remem-

bered poster appeared.   Under the pseudonym of 'Mjolnir', it carried the
slogan *Our Last Hope: Hitler* [112].

On 17 July 1936, the Government of Spain—itself the product of elections
of doubtful validity—was challenged by insurrection of units of the army
in Morocco.   The action, led by one General Francisco Franco Bahamonde,
spread to the mainland; within two days the whole country erupted in
civil war.

For decades torn by political and religious faction, Spain was now con-
vulsed by violence unparalleled in recent times.   In the two years and 254
days that ensued before Franco's final declaration of victory, both sides
committed acts of exceptional ruthlessness and brutality.   On the Government side, in pursuit of a merciless policy of anti-clericalism, there was
mass murder of bishops, priests and religious laity.   The Franco forces, in
saturation air attacks then without precedent, reduced the Basque town
of Guernica to rubble, killing many hundreds of its inhabitants.   The civil
war as a whole cost the lives of a million Spaniards.

Posters of the period that survive provide a graphic, if lopsided, image.
For whatever reason, the world's poster archives contain few, if any, from
the Franco side.   Research for the present collection has produced only the
last of Franco's war communiqués [166] *The War has Ended*.

One thing is certain: the Republican posters show a vision and vigour
perhaps unequalled before or since.   Poster propaganda for the Government was largely in the hands of the trades unions.   In Madrid, the Junta
Delegada de Defensa de Madrid under General Miaja operated a press and
propaganda bureau; during the 23 months siege of the city the artists' trade
union (SPBA) produced a stream of posters, many of them classics of their
kind.   From Valencia—to which the Government moved in November of
1936—came another stream.   Barcelona, seat of the semi-autonomous
Catalan Generalitat provided more posters—most of them in the language
of Catalunya.

If the 1930s were fraught with a sense of doom, they were undeniably the
golden age of the poster.   There can be little doubt that, in all its tragedy,
the Spanish civil war produced some of the best posters the world has
seen.   With a previous history of quiet mediocrity, the Spanish poster
suddenly reached the heights.

It must be conceded that they were not without their occasional banality;
there were some that were pale reflections of images of World War I:
And You—what have you done for victory? [47] is a throwback to the
multiple pointing fingers of 1914.   So is the home-front appeal of *Women!*

Work for the comrades at the Front [9]. But in the bravura and simplicity of *Join the Air Force* [1], *Strong men to the front!* [50] and *The Defence of Madrid is the Defence of Catalunya* [55] there is true poster greatness.

It is in the long-drawn conflict that the broadsheet style gives way to the pictorial poster. It is also in the long-drawn conflict that propaganda runs the full spectrum of appeal. From satire to monumentality, the Spanish Government posters covered a lot of ground. The multi-national profile in the *People's Army* poster [77], in its sense of strength and solidarity, has great impact. The satire of *Los Nacionales* [105] has impact no less powerful.

But the pictorial poster also reveals weaknesses. There can be few conflicting views on the implications of the *Discipline* poster [57], none at all in the case of that on looting: *Looting dishonours victory; Don't do it* [65]. (Mention of looting, pictorial or otherwise, is historically a bad omen for any cause. Among others who have publicly disclaimed and discouraged it are the Irish [100] and the Bavarians [85].)

Franco's *The War has Ended*, with its dateline *Burgos 1 April 1939*, must take its place with other proclamations of historical finality. Proclamations, though they may lack the pictorial appeal of the poster, make up in decisiveness what they lose in image. *The Union is Dissolved*, says a statement from the American South in 1851 [95]. *The Republic of Bavaria is Proclaimed* says Kurt Eisner in 1919 [79]. *The Dynasty of the Bourbons has Ceased to Reign*, says an aspiring Napoleon III in 1840 [168]. Says the Committee of National Liberation of the City of Milan on 26 April 1945: *For the Fascists a Single Choice: Surrender or Perish* [179].

As with other countries, Italy's posters of protest and revolution went for years without a picture; type-set broadsheets punctuated public life for many centuries. Garibaldi, one of the world's masters of insurrection, contributed his quota. They all reveal the authentic touch of dramatic immediacy. In a proclamation datelined *Bergamo 1839* [167] he conforms to the insurrectionary rule by calling on public functionaries to get on with their work without delay (excepting, as though by way of afterthought, those for whom the Government may have special instructions). The 1840s—as everywhere in Europe—produced a flurry of proclamations: from Milan in 1848 Garibaldi issued his appeal to the youth of Italy [146] *The Country Has Need of You . . . Let us Show Italy—and Europe . . . that we mean to Win!* This, a type-set version of Kitchener's pointing finger, successfully combines the approach of the authoritarian father-figure with that of the wild insurgent.

The *Your-Country-Needs-You* gambit, whether for revolution, for war, or for the status quo, had been a reliable rallying call in every country for generations. It was to be another hundred years before it began to lose its edge. By the 1950s there were indications that it had lost it altogether. Increasingly the appeal was for peace—and to class rather than country.

Spend for Peace, not for War [225]; *Free our Comrades from the Bosses' Prisons* [184]; *40,000 Workers in the Struggle; this is only the Beginning* [203]—Italian student-worker posters of the 'sixties echo the message of protest action in a score of countries. In their slogans, their images—even in their execution—these posters reflect an identity of attitude and internationality that makes hay of patriotism. Only occasionally are the old-style voices heard; says one poster, alone amid the rumpus, *Youth, Fight Against Blasphemy and Obscenity* [201]. Says another, a proclamation piece published by the Italian Social Movement, and speaking in unmistakably pre-revolutionary terms: 'Italian Social Movement does not accept, and cannot approve . . . opposition to the system which, both morally and materially damages the Forces of Order and the Armed Forces, injuring persons and occasioning harm to citizens. The Milan Federation of the Social Movement does not seek at this moment to take action, but. . . .' The full wording of the proclamation [180] leaves no doubt of the vintage or of the view of the Movement.

For the most part however, the contemporary poster of protest speaks the same language everywhere. Only in America is the accent noticeably different. Here, in place of heat-of-the-moment student panache, there is a more studied (though none the less biting) approach. The professional poster-maker, the graphic specialist and the US pop-art industry have combined to produce a new kind of poster altogether.

America has a long and solid history of dissent. The Founding Fathers, protesters even among Protestants, provide the keynote. In the Declaration of Independence, signed and delivered a century and a half later, the Americans have given the world a protest archetype; it is at once a condemnation, a call to unity and a proclamation of direct action. The Declaration differed only in detail from the draft prepared by Jefferson. (Among minor alterations was the omission of a denunciation of slavery.) The final document was adopted by Congress and read before the Army as a formal act of secession. Like Martin Luther's, it was a long document. Like his, it changed the course of human history.

But the omission of the reference to slavery was to prove significant. Rumbling beneath the surface for nearly eighty years, the slavery issue finally broke with Abraham Lincoln's words 'I believe this Government cannot endure permanently half slave and half free. . . . It will become all one thing or all the other'. Slavery—and the Civil War that was fought over it—is the subject matter of a major slice of American history; it is not surprisingly the subject matter of many of America's best-known posters of protest and revolution.

Neither the economies of the opposing sides, nor their technologies, permitted in the 1850s the production of pictorial posters; apart from the famous *God, Our Country and Liberty* [127] and a sprinkling of war-maps, most of the rest were broadsheets and proclamations. If a fraction more exuberant, they bore a striking resemblance in layout and treatment to their European contemporaries. More liberal in their use of exclamation marks than the conventional proclamation, they nevertheless adhered closely to the idiom. They contrived, for the most part, to finish with a signature. Even in the notice of the surrender of General Lee, which was in fact unsigned [134] a signature line *By Order of the People* appears. The line is curiously at odds with the totalitarian injunction that precedes it: '*Every Man, Woman and Child is hereby ordered to be on hand prepared to Sing and Rejoice. The crowd are expected to join in the singing of Patriotic Songs.*'

1917 was America's next poster burst—by this time fully pictorial. Of the posters of war and rumours of war, few can be described as posters of protest—except perhaps James Montgomery Flagg's pre-war *Wake Up America!* [26]. Published unofficially, this performed the same function in the United States as Britain's *Men! Your Country Needs You* poster [23]; it was a protest at the absence of conscription. The British poster, designed by an Australian and issued by the National Service League, appeared as early as 1911.

The full flower of American poster protest was to wait until the 1960s. By that time the poster in the United States had undergone a transformation. No longer simply a utilitarian item for the billboards, the poster had acquired a cachet as a collector's piece. Starting with posters of Europe's *belle époque*, and working their way through recent history to their own times, poster enthusiasts rediscovered the turn-of-the-century cult of poster collecting. With 'poster shops' opening in every other town, it was not long before demand outreached supply; soon poster reproductions appeared. In the late 1960s, by logical extension, posters were being designed specifically for the market; these, short-circuiting the due process of billboard display, went direct to walls of private living rooms.

Some manufacturers—for this is what they had now become—cashed in on an expanding market by commissioning 'genuine' posters by designers and offering them for actual billboard display to appropriate organisations and corporations. One poster for a certain zoo, for example, appeared on hoardings simply as 'fall-out' from a major printing for the poster shops. Thus, with the original role of the poster neatly inverted, it became first a collector's piece and secondarily an item of persuasion.

By the early 'seventies the poster—and the 'non-poster'—had become a cult object. Finally it found its own level in a vein of pop-art-cum-protest—an amalgam of interior décor and social comment. Typical of the genre is the *War is Good Business* design [224], a parody of nineteenth-century American private enterprise. And, as a parody of a parody, exploiting all angles at once, one commercial advertiser adopts the idiom (and perhaps the designer too?) in aid of anti-conformity whiskey sales [212].

For the designers who have emerged as protest specialists (Ungerer, Wilson, Thompson, Brown, Gilliam and others) there has been no shortage of subject matter. The Johnson era—Vietnam, conscription and race relations—provided much to be going on with; society as a whole provided the rest. Much of the material presented new versions of well-known publicity images, using montage and collage techniques to convey a message with a twist [211]. Much of it is designedly unattractive [215]. All of it is bitter.

In general level, the American poster of protest makes up in expertise what it may lack in a sense of immediacy. Only rarely does there appear the unmistakable mark of the popular will—the common touch. Nearest in its sense of spontaneity is the poster for the pacifist organisation Women Strike for Peace [218]; in slogan, treatment and presentation (the design is printed on card and carried in procession by children), this poster combines charm with emotional impact. Where other designs show signs of contrivance, here is a convincing air of throw-away effortlessness.

If the contemporary trend in social and political protest is sarcasm, in other fields it is decidedly not. In protest against aircraft noise, against vivisection and cruelty to animals, against swearing and drinking, against pit closures, tax increases, and a host of peripheral ills, satire is noticeably absent. Grim-faced as a call to the barricades, the appeal of Britain's Royal Society for the Prevention of Cruelty to Animals is real and earnest [155, 156, 157]. So is that of the International Council Against Bullfighting [154] and the Pit Ponies Protection Society [152]. It is for the major issues—war, freedom and the H-bomb—that the tongue-in-cheek approach finally appears. *War is Good Business* expresses the mood of a new generation of acid comment. Similarly—and surely with irreducible brevity—the anti-H-bomb syllable: *OOPS!* [220].

Britain, home of the side-show individualist and the minority society-for-this-that-and-the-other, has added much to the poster archive. If she has produced little in the way of actual revolution, in protest she has offered more than the average. With a freedom of expression that her citizens are inclined either to ignore or to take for granted, Britain has a long tradition of minority indulgence. The 'illegal' poster, not unknown elsewhere [216], is in Britain a rarity. (So is its corollary—illegal defacement of the poster. Defacement, as in the occupied France example [171/2], has in many situations constituted a punishable offence. In Russia in 1917 a number of revolutionary posters bore the small-print footnote: *Anyone removing or covering up this poster commits a counter-revolutionary act*.) In Britain, apart from instances of alleged obscenity, there have been only a few cases of suppression by authority. *Wars will cease when men refuse to fight* [22] was one of these. Published by the Peace Pledge Union shortly before World War II, the charge against this poster rested on a nice point of British law: did the words *What are you going to do about it?* the poster's secondary slogan, constitute an offence? Was it an incitement to disaffection amongst the public at large (which was not an offence) or incitement to disaffection amongst His Majesty's Armed Forces (which, in 1939, was)? To whom was the poster addressed? If to members of the Forces—or if there was a possibility of soldiers, sailors or airmen seeing the poster—this was a criminal offence, and those who published and displayed it in time of war faced imprisonment under Defence Regulation 39a/1.

It must be said that the Peace Pledge Union was itself uncertain of its conscience in the matter. The question for them to answer was: had they meant the poster for civilian-only display? And if they had, where was the logic in appealing only to civilians to stop fighting?

After a searching of hearts and a weighing of the balance of positions, the Peace Pledge Union came to the conclusion that, when the poster had originally appeared in 1938, it had been directed to civilians. But in view of possible misinterpretation 'in present circumstances' they formally withdrew the poster.

They were formally discharged. The whole operation was conducted in a spirit of gentle reasonableness. Said the magistrate, at the end of the proceedings, 'I know that I am dealing with men who . . . are reputable citizens in the highest sense of the word. Some people may think them wrong-headed. I do not express any view in regard to that, but I believe them to be honourable men. . . .'

Newest-comer to the poster of protest in the United Kingdom is Wales. Home rule, a resurgent issue in many areas in the 'sixties, has produced slogan campaigns in a variety of languages—among them, in Europe, Basque, Walloon, Cornish and Breton. So far only Wales appears to have produced actual posters. Casting their message alternately in Welsh and English as convenient, much of the stress of Welsh protest has been on water. Much of it is also on irreverence for Charles, heir to the throne of England. Water from the Welsh mountains ('one of Wales's significant exports') is a gratuitous source of supply for a number of English towns; letterpress posters [160, 161, 162, 163] make the point in English. The young man from Buckingham Palace ('one of Wales's insignificant imports') is a source of irritation.   The posters of nationalist Robat Gruffud's printing press [164, 165] say it in Welsh.

From Cuba, in terms distinctly more direct, comes a poster series in a number of languages at once.   Here, in a pledge of solidarity with dissent in various parts of the world, Cuba celebrates the coming of liberation— past, present and future.   *Each year by which America's liberation may be hastened will mean millions of children rescued from death*, says the caption to a poster image of children in a shanty town [125].   Centre-point of the series is an exercise in dynamic wordlessness [126]—the Che Guevara image, multipally magnified and merged on a background of a map of the South American continent.   A micro-caption notes the dateline: *Day of the Heroic Guerrilla, October 8.*

The Cuban revolutionary poster owes nothing to its forebears, native or foreign.   In an idiom entirely its own it emerges on the poster scene as an entity fully evolved—original, authoritative and completely independent.

Among posters of revolution, Cuba's are unique in one special respect: whereas elsewhere the weapons of battle are portrayed as dramatic—often as aggressively ugly—in the posters of Cuba they are made to look pretty. It is with a shock that the eye lights on a decorative background [123] and takes in a composition made up of silhouettes of bullets, rifles and sub- machine guns.   In another poster [124] a decorative emblem on the fore- head of an Angolan warrior reveals itself as a hand-grenade.   The symbol of the publishing agency, OSPAAAL (Organisation for Solidarity of the Peoples of Africa, Asia and Latin America) appears as an imprint on the posters; it features a decorative motif of world, hand and gun.

Unlike those of Cuba, the visual idiom of the posters of the People's Republic of China breaks little or no new ground.   While rejecting the image of classical 'chinoiserie' the revolutionary Chinese poster turns not to a mode of its own but to conventions of the outside world.   In the muscu- lar heroes of its wide-screen action pieces [61] and in the larger-than-life exuberance of its Red Book holders and paper-tiger scarers [58, 59] there is more than a trace of the vintage Hollywood billboard.

Of their genre, they are superbly competent. Although to the Western eye they may be more redolent of the 'forties than the turn of the 'sixties, many of them have a powerful impact.   Most of them feature longer or shorter extracts from the sayings of Chairman Mao; for the most part they successfully survive a punishing overload of wording.

Classically, in protest or revolution, it has been the Poster that has come readiest to hand for the ordinary man.   It is one of the few media of mass communication that the average man can manage for himself throughout—thinking up his own ideas, drawing them out on paper, and posting them up for everyone to see. The home-made poster was a notable feature of the Russia of 1917; it served then—and it still serves—a double role; it is not only a bearer of a message, it is a gesture of irreverence to the walls it covers. In Russia it was used almost as a physical obliteration of the structure of the old régime. In China's cultural revolution it has played a similar role; in the background to the scene in the poster *Aim straight; Hit hard* [102] the principle appears in practice.

In the streets of France in May 1968 it appeared again. The students of Paris, for weeks in occupation of the buildings of their colleges, started poster production in a big way. They produced over 350 different designs —in all, some 120,000 printed posters. In doing so they brought the poster to a new phase—back to where it had come in, in the hands of do-it-yourself dissent. But this time it was not on a Martin Luther basis; this time it was in quantity. The effect on the walls, the monuments and the public buildings of Paris was noticeable; in parts, obliteration was almost complete.

It was an operation without precedent. With only rudimentary equipment, and with almost as little in the way of production discipline, a total of 200 students got together to set up an *ad hoc* poster factory in the building of the *Beaux Arts*. Pooling their poster ideas, thrashing out slogans and 'angles' in open discussion, fashioning and refashioning designs by popular approval, the students produced posters almost as soon as they had thought of them.

A keynote throughout was topicality. Working from a 'text-board' (a central display on which themes and phrases of the day were posted up as raw material) students formulated poster-ideas around the news. Said one poster, appearing shortly after Cohn-Bendit had been expelled from the country as 'undesirable', *We are all undesirable!* Said another, after police had used armoured vehicles to disperse demonstrators and strikers, *Light wages; heavy armour.* Student comment—often witty, invariably bitter—was on the streets almost hour by hour.

The idiom of the French student poster was a direct product of its environment. Carried out in simple lithography or silk-screen stencil (occasionally in wood- or lino-cut) it was the quickest possible statement of an urgent and heart-felt message. In one colour only, with images restricted in the main to simple solid areas of colour, the strength of the poster lay largely in its basic idea. The design was approached not as an exercise in applied aesthetics but as an expression of a moment of history. Perhaps none of the designs expresses the idiom better than *Ceder un peu, c'est beaucoup capituler* [195]—in visual and verbal economy and in the burden of its message, it epitomises the month of May 1968.

By design, or by environmental coincidence, the idiom has appeared elsewhere. So have the concepts it conveys. That the results may have been significantly less telling may be due to a variety of reasons: perhaps pressures have been less; perhaps conviction has been weaker; perhaps literary and cultural traditions have been different. Though they partake of something of the quality of the French designs, those from Italy [193, 196, 203] and from Sweden [217], Germany [178] and Britain [89, 199] have nothing of the biting expertise of their predecessors.

Stemming from the Paris students' 1968 example, *ad hoc* poster production units appeared in a number of countries. These, working on an informal cooperative basis, supplied simple printing facilities free of charge to protest movements of all kinds. 'Customers' range from strikers' action groups to Tenants' Associations. Often the customers design and produce the posters themselves, using the skills and equipment of the volunteer 'specialists'. One such poster workshop in London, complete with production discussion groups and a 'slogan wall' *à la Beaux Arts*, has a broadsheet advertising itself [228]. 'The workshop', said a manifesto that appeared on its walls when it opened, 'is a tool for counter-information at the service of the class-struggle: solidarity with industrial, student and tenant strikers, and liberation fronts all over the world. You are invited to participate with information, ideas, slogans, archetypes, designs, and the actual printing of the posters in silk screen. The projects will be voted upon by the assembly on the spot.'

The Poster has passed through a number of clearly discernible historical stages. It has served variously as *vox Dei, vox populi, and vox domini*; it has served as weapon of war, of commerce, of disaffection, irreverence, and seduction. It has been by turns a nuisance, a necessity, a menace— and, in the era of commercial television, a premature bygone. As it settled down in the late 'sixties to being a cult-object, suddenly it became everybody's protest stand-by. In the 1970s there are signs that the Poster may be starting a second time round.

INDEX

ACKNOWLEDGEMENTS

Among the many organisations and individuals who have helped in the preparation of
this book, the author and publisher would especially like to thank: Mr Max Alexander;
Association of Members of Hornsey College of Art; 'Avant-Garde'; Mrs Balfour, The
Economist, London; Mr John Bartlett, Wilberforce House, Hull; British Union for the
Abolition of Vivisection; Mrs Bruna Broggio, Edizioni Bompiani, Milan; Mrs Janey Buchan;
Campaign for Nuclear Disarmament, London; Mr Peter Celiz; Mr A. W. Cloo; The
Cuban Embassy, London; Mr John Dudman; Mr O. H. Edwards; Mr Harold C. Feldt;
Miss Jasmine Gale, BPC Publishing Ltd; Mrs Solveig Gervin, Steen Hasselbalchs Forlag
A/S, Copenhagen; The Goldsmiths' Library; Mr Robat Gruffudd, Y Lolfa, Wales; Mrs
Johanna Harrison; Mr George Him; Housman's Bookshop, London; The Imperial War
Museum; Information Office, Spanish Embassy, London; Instituto Culturale Italiano,
London; The International Council against Bullfighting; Italian Communist Party; Mrs
Sophie Johnson; The John Judkyn Memorial, Bath; Mr Ronald Julyan; Mr Stan Krol; The
Labour Party; Mr Kenneth Lo; Mr Willy de Majo; Colonel J. R. P. Montgomery, the Anti-
Slavery Society; The Morning Star, London; Movimento Nazionale Antiblasfemo;
Movimento Sociale Italiano; Museo del Risorgimento Nazionale di Milano; National
Library of Ireland; National Library of Scotland; Mr Enzo Nizza, Edizioni La Pietra; Miss
Freda Nuell, Christian Action; Pit Ponies Protection Society; Plaid Cymru; Mr John
Rothstein, The Marx Memorial Library; The Royal Society for the Prevention of Cruelty
to Animals; Miss Agnes Scheuermann; Society of Friends, London; Miss Myrtle Solomon,
Peace Pledge Union; Mr Ken Sprague; Mr Peter Suchodolski; Professor Hugh Thomas;
Mr Turner, John Johnson Collection, The Bodleian Library; L'Unità, Milan; United States
Information Service; The University of London Library; Victoria & Albert Museum, Lon-
don; Mr B. Weinreb; The Wiener Library; Mr S. John Woods; Young Communist League.

POSTERS OF PROTEST AND REVOLUTION

P.S.U.

PER A AIXAFAR EL FEIXISME

INGRESSEU A L'AVIACIO

EDITAT PEL SINDICAT DE DIBUIXANTS PROFESSIONALS U.G.T.

GRAF. ULTRA S.A. CORCEGA, 220 - BARCELONA

1 SPAIN c. 1937

Anonymous
*To fight Fascism
— join the Airforce*

HAVE YOU GIVEN LIFE
TO YOUR SON THAT
HE MAY KILL THE SONS
OF OTHER MOTHERS?
MOTHERS!

2 BRITAIN c. 1938
   Giele Roelofs

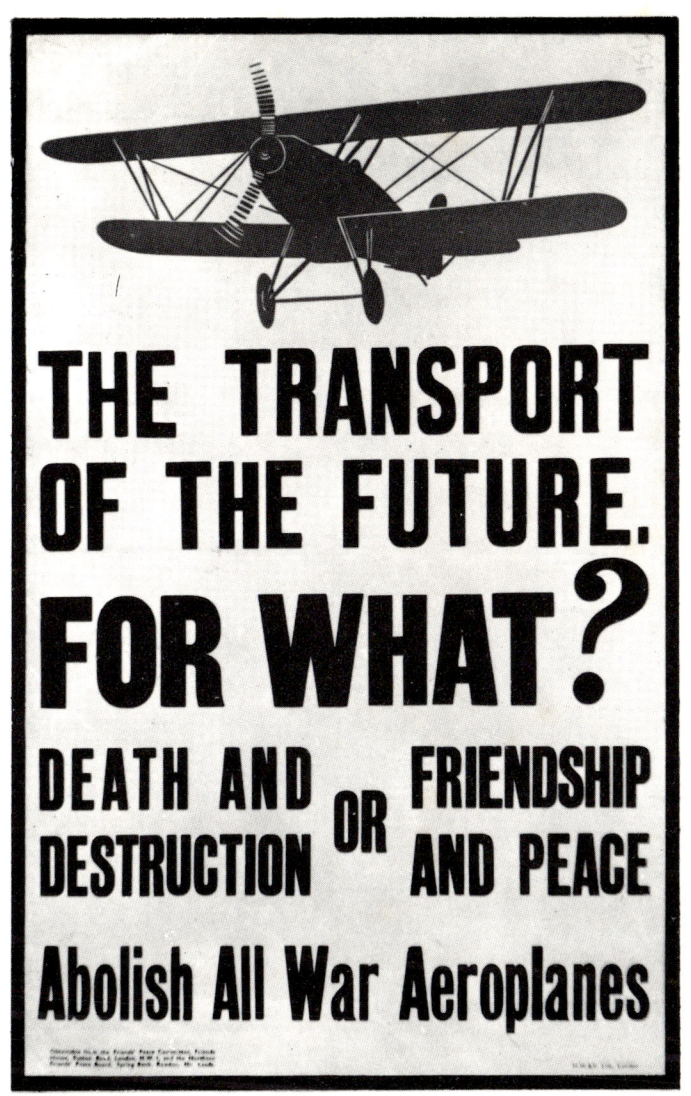

3 BRITAIN c. 1933

Anonymous

4 SPAIN c. 1937

Anonymous
*More men, more arms,
more munitions
— to the Front*

5 GERMANY 1928

A. Keil
*Mothers! Was it for this
that your children were born?
Sign* [the petition] *against
battlecruisers and war!*

6 GERMANY 1958
Anonymous
*No experiments... no atom testing;
we protest against the
nuclear arming of the Bundeswehr*

7 GERMANY 1924
Käthe Kollwitz
No more war

ИМПЕРИАЛИЗМ— ЭТО ВОЙНА!

8 RUSSIA c. 1966
V. Briskin
Imperialism is war!

9 SPAIN c. 1937

Anonymous

Women! Work for the comrades at the front

10 GERMANY c. 1919

Siegmund von Suchodolski

We tolerate no anarchy;
we will protect women and children

11 RUSSIA c. 1933

Anonymous

Pass on the experience of age to youth

12 RUSSIA 1923

Anonymous

*In destroying Capitalism the proletariat
will also destroy prostitution;
prostitution is the great evil of humanity;
workers, honour and respect the woman worker*

13 BRITAIN 1918/19
David Wilson / WFB

14 AUSTRIA 1919
Vèrles

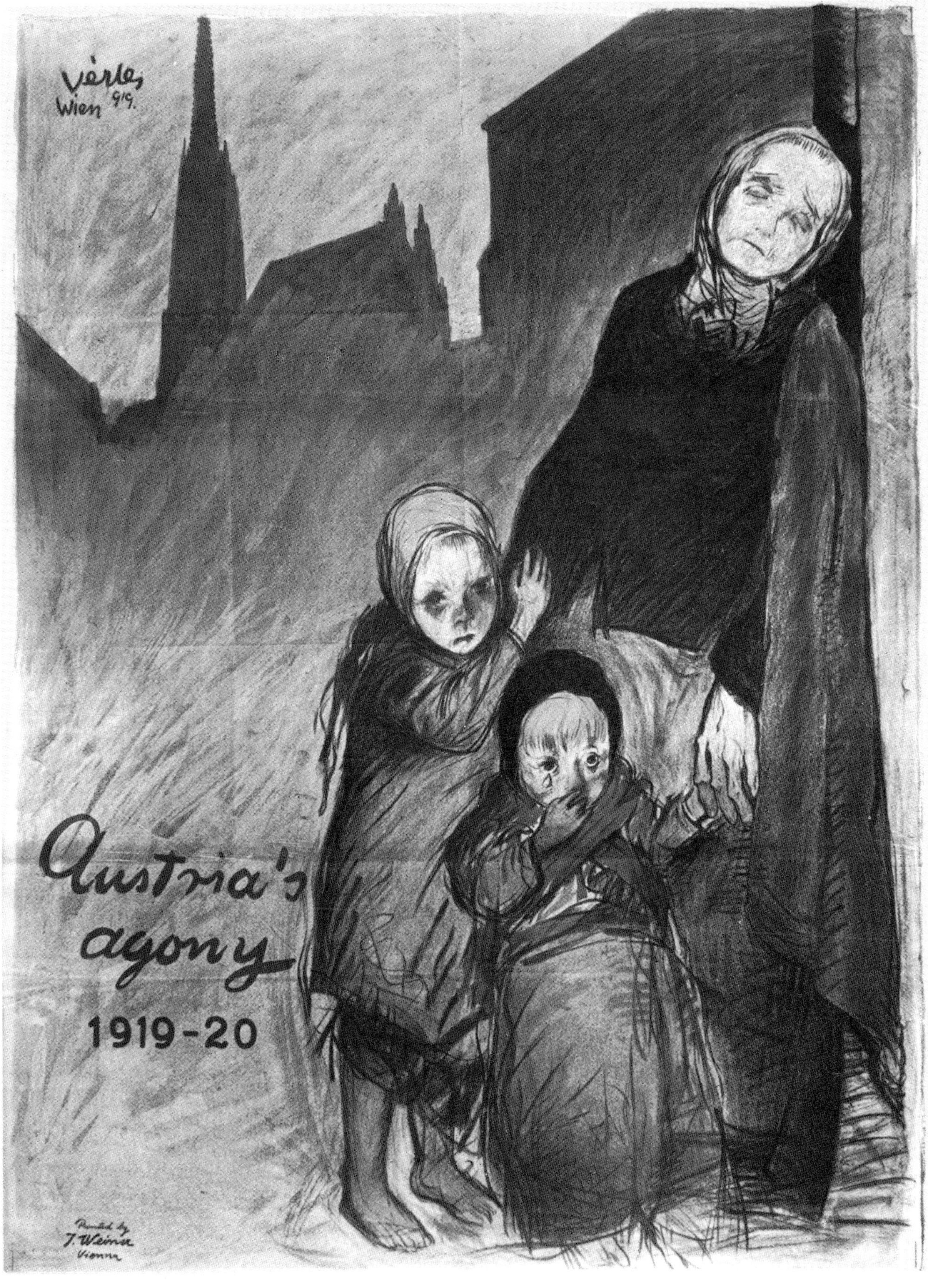

15 GERMANY 1914

Karl Maria Stadler
Women's Day; Votes for women!

16 GERMANY 1918

Schnackenberg
Anarchy — friend of reaction and famine

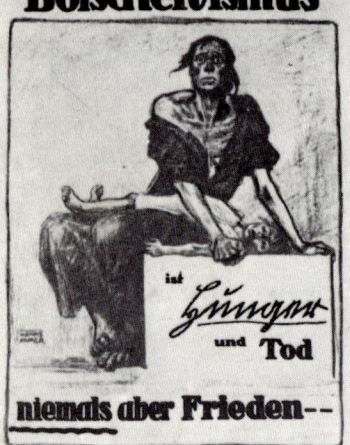

19 GERMANY
c. 1919

Hans Anker
Bolshevism means hunger and death — peace it never is

20 BRITAIN 1911

Anonymous
(Suffragette poster)

WHY WORRY ABOUT
PORTUGAL
IN
ENGLISH PRISONS
ENGLISH PEOPLE
ARE BEING
TORTURED
NOW !!!

17 POLAND 1921

Anonymous

Mother, remember me. Vote for Poland

18 GERMANY 1918

Martha Jäger

Your children need Peace and Bread; Women, VOTE!

21 GERMANY 1930

K.

Women, this is your role in the 'Third Reich'

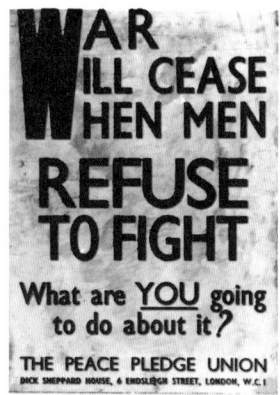

22 BRITAIN 1938
Anonymous

23 BRITAIN 1911
Meeson-Coates

26 AMERICA 1916
James Montgomery Flagg

27 GERMANY 1919
(.....?)
The Homeland in danger!

24 GERMANY 1919
Anonymous
Bavarians, the Bolshevik is about!
Out with him on election day!
Bavarian People's Party

25 BRITAIN 1942
Anonymous

29 GERMANY 1919
Safis
Bolshevism means
a world
drenched in blood

28 GERMANY 1919
(.....?)
The Homeland is
in danger!

30 GERMANY 1953
Anonymous
All Marxist roads
lead to Moscow.
Vote CDU

TO ARMS!
RALLY FOR THE RIGHT!
Recruits Wanted
For THREE MONTHS SERVICE, IN
COMPANY A
GRAY RESERVES
CAPT. CHARLES S. SMITH.
ARMORY,
810 MARKET STREET,
UP STAIRS.

31 USA 1861
Anonymous

ANTI-CONSCRIPTION PLEDGE.

The following is a copy of the Pledge:—

"Denying the right of the British Government to enforce Compulsory Service in this Country *we pledge ourselves solemnly to one another to resist Conscription* by the most effective means at our disposal."

32 IRELAND 1916
Anonymous

YESTERDAY-THE TRENCHES

TO-DAY–UNEMPLOYED

38 BRITAIN c. 1922
G. Spencer Pryse

39 RUSSIA 1921
D. S. Moor
(Dmitri Stakheyevitch Orlov)
Help!
(Volga Famine Aid)

40 RUSSIA 1921

I. Simakov

Remember the hungry

41 SPAIN c. 1937

Anonymous
*Farmer! Victory needs
your effort. Help us!*

43 RUSSIA 1930

(.....?)
*Comrade! Prepare, as a Bolshevik,
for a 'shock-tactic sowing campaign'*

42 SPAIN c. 1937

Anonymous
*Getting in the harvest
is as good as the
enemy beaten in battle*

44 RUSSIA 1920

D. S. Moor
*You — have you enrolled as
a volunteer?*

45 HUNGARY 1919

Anonymous
YOU! Counter-revolutionary,
skulking in the shadows,
spreading despondency — TREMBLE!

46 RUSSIA c. 1923

Anonymous
YOU — not yet a
member of the cooperative
— JOIN NOW!

47 SPAIN c. 1937

Anonymous
And you?
— what have you done
for victory?

48 RUSSIA c. 1921

Anonymous
YOU — have you helped
the hungry children of the Volga?
HURRY UP, THEN!

49 RUSSIA 1919

A. Apsit
*We will defend Petrograd
with our lifeblood*

51 RUSSIA 1919

A. Petrov (A. Apsit)
Forward, in defence of the Urals

50 SPAIN c. 1937

Anonymous
Strong men — to the Front!

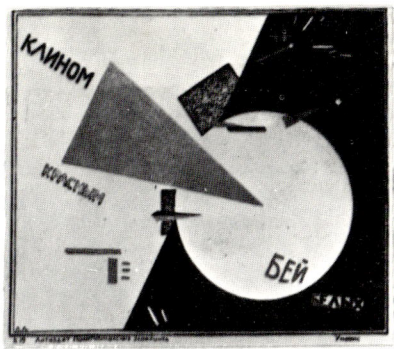

52 RUSSIA 1920
Lazar Lizitsky
With the Red wedge, divide the Whites!

55 SPAIN c. 1937
Anonymous
*The defence of Madrid
is the defence
of Catalunya*

53 HUNGARY 1919
Dankó
Join the Red Army

56 SPAIN c. 1937
Anonymous
*Soldiers
of the Republic,
ATTACK!*

54 SPAIN c. 1937
Anonymous
*More men! More arms!
More munitions!*

57 SPAIN c. 1937
Anonymous
*Discipline,
the only command
— byword of Victory!*

58 CHINA 1966

Anonymous
*Chairman Mao is
the Red Son
of our Hearts*

59 CHINA c. 1966

Anonymous
*Our victory is assured.
The Hong Kong British
are certain to be defeated.
Do not insult the
people of China.
Chairman Mao says:
'With firm determination,
no deviation,
no fear of difficulties
— forward to final victory.
Imperialists and
Reactionaries
are paper tigers!'*

60 CHINA 1966

Anonymous
*The thoughts of Mao
Tse Tung
are your weapons...
— to expose wrongs
— to criticise wrongs
— to overthrow wrongs.
No retreat! Total victory!*

61 CHINA 1966

Anonymous
*American Imperialists — get out of South Vietnam
— out of Africa — out of Asia — out of Taiwan
— out of the Congo — get out of Latin America*

美帝国主义从拉丁美洲滚出去

美 帝 国 主 义 从 它 霸 占 的 一 切 地
U.S. Imperialism Must Get Out of All Places It Occupie
L'impérialisme américain hors de tous les territoires qu'il
¡Fuera los imperialistas norteamericanos de todos los terr

美帝国主义从越南南方滚出去!

美帝国主义从非洲滚出去! 美帝国主义从亚洲滚出

美帝国主义从刚果(利)滚出去!

美帝国主义从台湾滚出去!

滚 出 去

...pe!

...s que ocupan!

人民美术出版社出版·北京
国际书店发行

62 RUSSIA c. 1919

D. S. Moor (Dmitri Stakheyevitch Orlov)

A Sacred Undertaking
(At the foot of the poster
appear the words of the Act of Commitment
for entrants to the Red Army)

63 RUSSIA 1920

Alexei Alexandrovitch Radakhov

The illiterate is a blind man; failure and disaster await him

64 RUSSIA 1920

Anonymous

Comrade, redoubling our energies, from across the serried ranks of arms, over the forests of bayonets, we joyously salute the third anniversary of the October Revolution. This is the guarantee of our coming victory: we need never more be slaves. Through temporary setbacks and tribulations we march together into the bright kingdom of Work. The Dragon of Imperialism, sundered with the sword of the Proletariat, breathes its last. Long live the World Soviet Socialist Federal Republic. Long live its power!

65 SPAIN 1938

Anonymous

Looting dishonours victory.
Don't do it

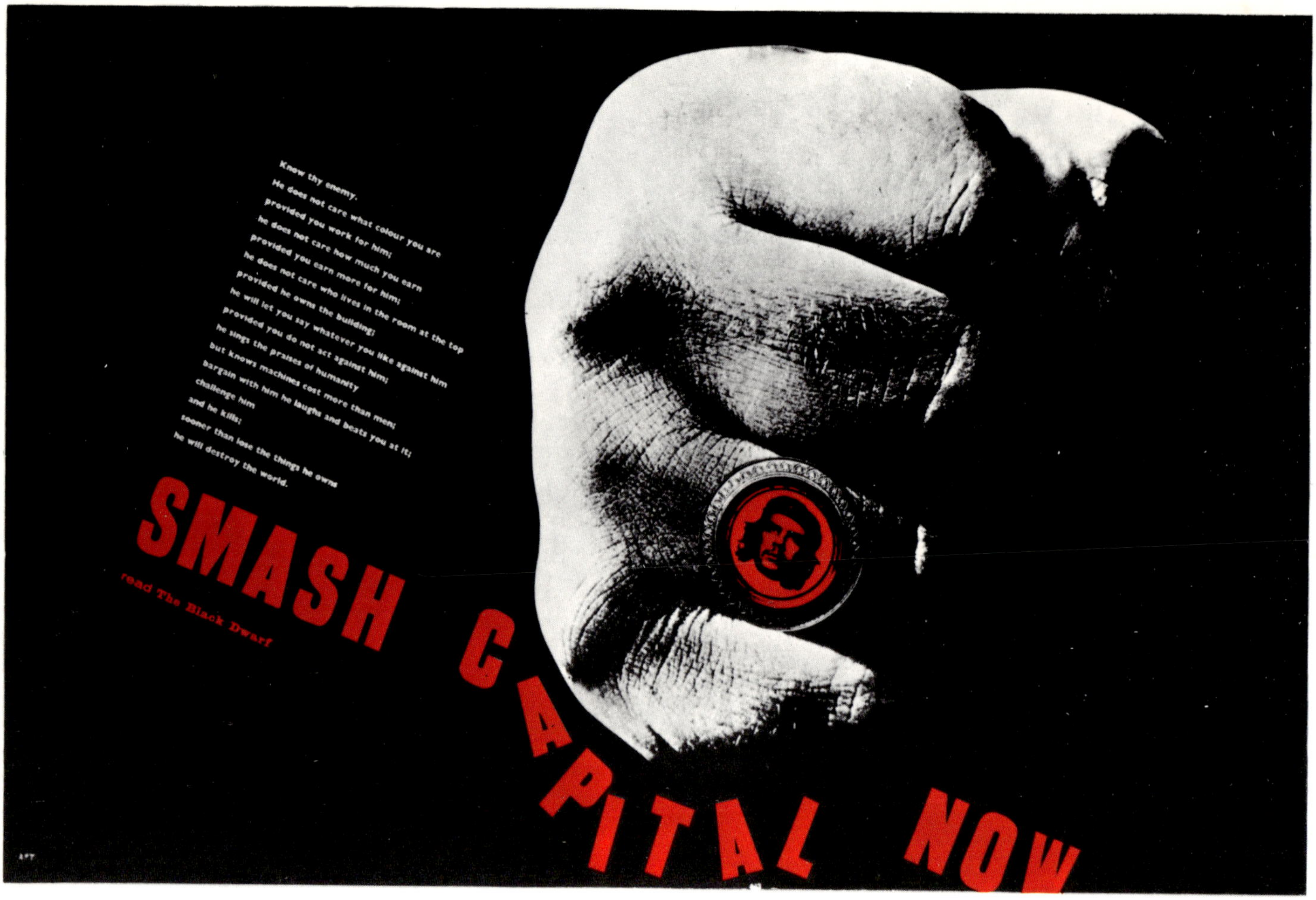
Know thy enemy.
He does not care what colour you are
provided you work for him;
he does not care how much you earn
provided you earn more for him;
he does not care who lives in the room at the top
provided he owns the building;
he will let you say whatever you like against him
provided you do not act against him;
he sings the praises of humanity
but knows machines cost more than men;
bargain with him he laughs and beats you at it;
challenge him
and he kills;
sooner than lose the things he owns
he will destroy the world.
SMASH CAPITAL NOW
read The Black Dwarf

66 BRITAIN 1968
Anonymous

67 RUSSIA c. 1947
(.....?)
Give quality!

ДАЙ
КАЧЕСТВО!

68 GERMANY 1920
Safis
Free us from Red fetters!
German People's Party!

Von roten Ketten macht uns frei
Allein die
Deutsche Volkspartei
Wahlkreisverband Berlin Zimmerstr. 72-74

69 GERMANY 1920
Anonymous
Vote 'Spartacus'!
(The Spartacist Party represented
Germany's extreme left in 1920)

Wählt Spartakus

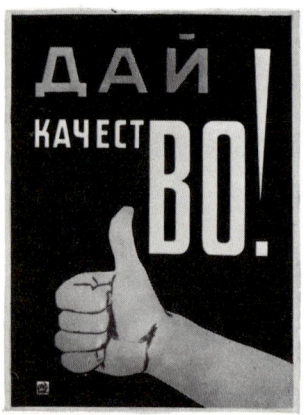

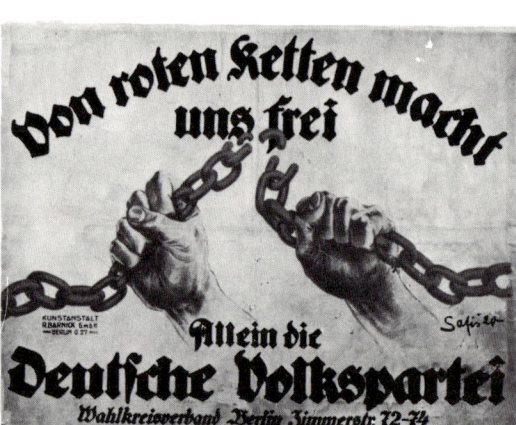

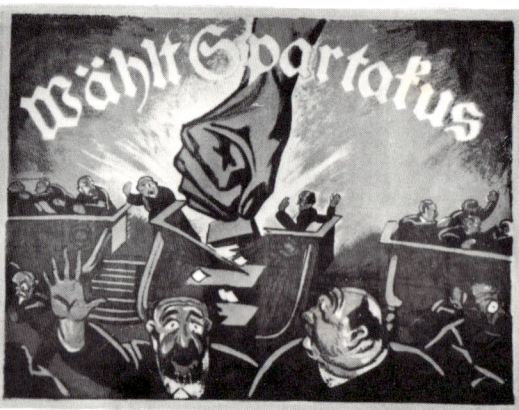

JUNTA DELEGADA DE DEFENSA
DE MADRID

DELEGACION DE PROPAGANDA Y PRENSA

LA GARRA DEL INVASOR ITALIANO PRETENDE ESCLAVIZARNOS

SINDICATO PROFESIONALES BELLAS ARTES U.G.T.

RIVADENEYRA C.S.-MADRID

70 SPAIN 1938
Anonymous
The claw of the
Italian invader seeks
to enslave us

JUNTA DELEGADA DE DEFENSA
DE MADRID

DELEGACION DE PROPAGANDA Y PRENSA

Ayudad a **MADRID**
SUFRIDO Y HEROICO

71 SPAIN 1937

Anonymous
*Help Madrid
— enduring... heroic...*

72 GERMANY 1928

H. Busch
*National Socialist
— otherwise the sacrifice
was in vain*

73 SPAIN 1937

Anonymous
Syndicalist party

74 FRANCE c. 1944

R. Louvat

75 SPAIN c. 1937

Anonymous
Forward!

76 GERMANY 1919

Alois Seidl
*Enlist in the Army
Regiment, Munich*

77 SPAIN c. 1937

Anonymous
*All militias united in
the People's Army*

Anonymous
*The personnel of the Royal Post and Telegraph Office are
required to take up their duties immediately.*
— Workers' and Soldiers' Council

79 GERMANY 1918

Anonymous
*Proclamation: Comrades! In order to rebuild after years
of destruction, the people have taken power from the civil
and military authorities and have taken over the Government. The Republic of Bavaria is hereby proclaimed.
Supreme power rests with the Workers', Soldiers' and
Peasants' Soviets elected by the people and installed pro-
visionally until final popular representation has been
constituted. The Soviets have legislative power. The entire
garrison has placed its services at the disposal of the
Republican Government. The High Command of the
Directorate of the Police are subject to our orders. The
dynasty of the Wittelsbachs is deposed. Long live the
Republic!*
— For the Workers' and Soldiers' Soviet: Kurt Eisner

80 GERMANY 1918

Anonymous
*Proclamation by the New Chancellor Ebert: Warning: Law and
Order! Citizens! The former Chancellor, Prince Max von Baden,
has invested in me the powers of conducting the business of
Chancellor... I ask all of you for your support in the difficult tasks
ahead of us. You know to what extent the War has jeopardised
the task of feeding the people - a task the successful fulfilment of
which is the basis of all political life. The political revolution must
not be allowed to interfere with feeding the nation: it must remain
the prime duty of everybody in town and country to support the
production of food and its distribution to the towns rather than to
prevent it. Lack of food means looting, misery and want for
everybody. The poorest would be affected most, industrial workers
hit hardest. Everybody who interferes with food, or other essential
goods or with the means of transport needed for their distribution,
commits a grave offence against the community. Citizens! I ask all
of you to leave the streets! Maintain law and order.*
— Berlin, 9th November 1918. Chancellor Ebert

81 GERMANY 1919

Anonymous

Workers! The fight against the bourgeoisie and the traitors of the proletariat has blazed into full action. With your first assault you have conquered important positions. Complete victory can only be achieved and consolidated if the armed struggle is continued without let-up. Workers, join the General Strike! Do not resume work until full victory has been gained! Everything is at stake! Your future is at stake! The victory of the proletarian world revolution is at stake!
Excluded from the strike are Railway, Post Office, Telegraph and Telephone Workers and also workers and staff on essential production, gas, water and electricity plants, staff concerned with preparing and paying out wages or employed in social welfare. Restaurants are likewise excluded from the strike for the time being.
— Executive of the Workers' and Soldiers' Soviets of Munich.
Munich, 14th April 1919

82 GERMANY 1919

Wustrau
Come on, Comrade! Join the Tüllmann Detachment

83 FRANCE 1968

Anonymous
*Support the occupied
factories for a
People's Victory*

85 GERMANY 1919

Anonymous
*Announcement. Whoever commits acts against the present Government or incites others to commit such acts, or robs, loots or steals, will be shot — according to ordinances concerning the state of siege and to be published later. Munich, 21st February 1919.
— Niekisch, Executive Officer of the Workers' Soviet; Simon, for the Executive Council of the Soldiers' Soviet; Staimer, President of Police; Dürr, Garrison Commander.*

84 FRANCE 1968

Anonymous
*French and Immigrant
workers united*

86 FRANCE 1968 Anon.
People's Power

87 FRANCE 1968 Anon.
Farmer, stand by your sons

88 ITALY 1969 Anon.
Workers, students — united

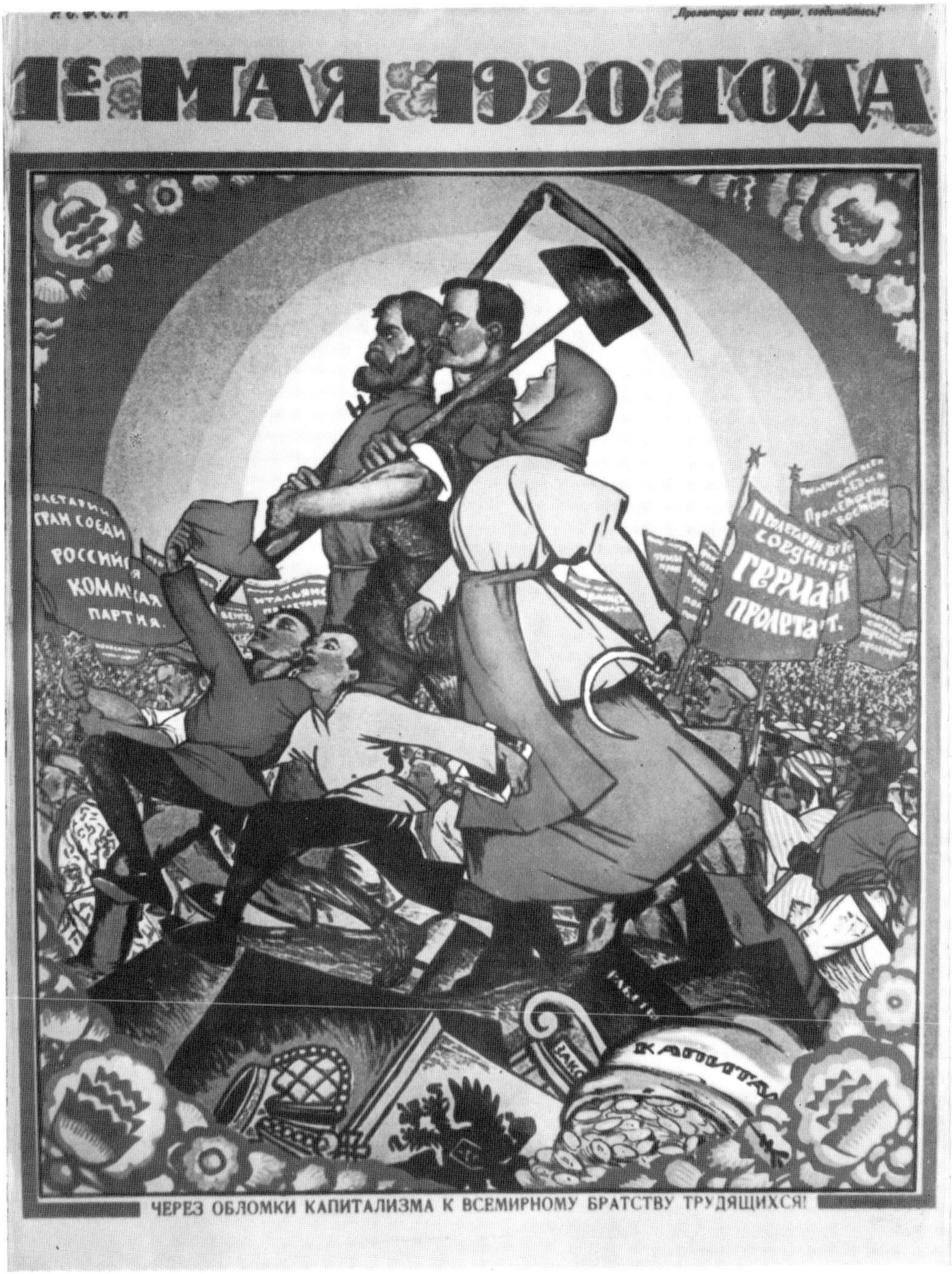

91 FRANCE 1968 Anonymous
May 1968 — beginning of a long struggle

92 RUSSIA 1920 S. Ivanov
May 1. Long live the Workers' Festival

89 BRITAIN 1969
Anonymous

90 RUSSIA 1920
Nikolai Kocherghin
On the ruins of capitalism towards worldwide brotherhood of the workers

93 FRANCE 1968
Anonymous
Unity: workers, farmers

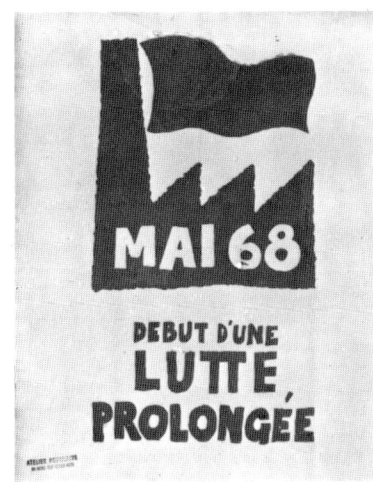

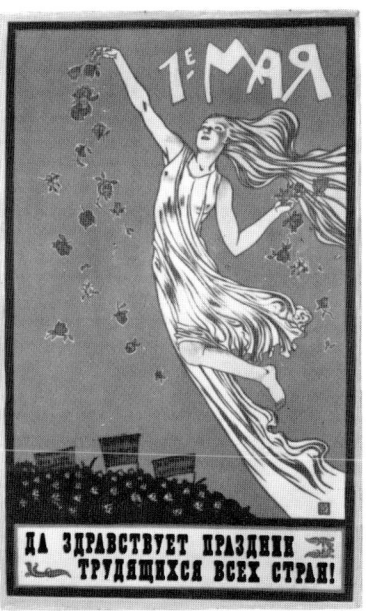

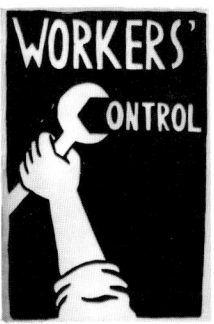

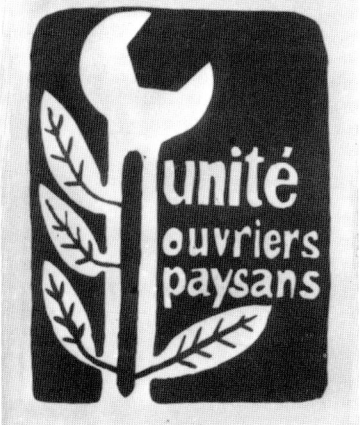

WE HAVE
TAXES
Upon every Article which enters into the Mouth, or covers the Back, or is placed under the Foot.

TAXES
Upon every thing which is pleasant to See, Hear, Feel, Smell and Taste.

TAXES
Upon Warmth, Light, and Locomotion.

TAXES
On every thing on Earth, and the Waters under the Earth; on every thing that comes from Abroad, or is grown at Home.

EARL GREY.

TAXES
On the Raw Material, and every thing that is added to it by the Industry of Man.

TAXES
On the Sauce which pampers Man's Appetite, and the Drug which restores him to Health.

TAXES
On the ERMINE which decorates the JUDGE, and the ROPE which hangs the CRIMINAL.

TAXES
ON THE BRASS NAILS OF THE COFFIN, AND THE RIBBANDS OF THE BRIDE:
AT
BED OR AT *BOARD, SITTING* OR *LAYING,*
WE MUST PAY!
The SCHOOL BOY whips his TAXED TOP; and the BEARDLESS YOUTH manages his TAXED HORSE with a TAXED BRIDLE on a TAXED ROAD;
AND
The Dying Englishman
Pouring his Medicine, which has paid SEVEN PER CENT., into a TAXED SPOON which has paid THIRTY PER CENT.
THROWS HIMSELF BACK ON A CHINTZ BED WHICH HAS PAID 22 PER CENT.
MAKES HIS WILL,
In which he is assisted by a Lawyer who pays a TAX of £120. for the privilege of so doing:
HIS WHOLE PROPERTY IS THEN TAXED FROM TWO TO TEN PER CENT.
When placed in his Coffin, the Shroud which covers him pays a Tax of 22 per Cent.—His Virtues are recorded on TAXED MARBLE.
HE IS THEN GATHERED TO HIS FATHERS,
TO BE
TAXED NO MORE!!!

94 BRITAIN c. 1825

Anonymous

CHARLESTON
MERCURY
EXTRA:

Passed unanimously at 1.15 o'clock, P. M. December 20th, 1860.

AN ORDINANCE

To dissolve the Union between the State of South Carolina and other States united with her under the compact entitled "The Constitution of the United States of America."

We, the People of the State of South Carolina, in Convention assembled, do declare and ordain, and it is hereby declared and ordained,

That the Ordinance adopted by us in Convention, on the twenty-third day of May, in the year of our Lord one thousand seven hundred and eighty-eight, whereby the Constitution of the United States of America was ratified, and also, all Acts and parts of Acts of the General Assembly of this State, ratifying amendments of the said Constitution, are hereby repealed; and that the union now subsisting between South Carolina and other States, under the name of "The United States of America," is hereby dissolved.

THE
UNION
IS
DISSOLVED!

95 USA 1860

Anonymous

l'ALARME

Président d'Honneur
Mr Raymond POINCARÉ

Société Française d'Action
CONTRE L'ALCOOLISME

Ce que nous n'avons pū faire l'Alcool le fera

AUX FRANÇAISES
ET AUX JEUNES FRANÇAIS

L'Alcool est votre ennemi aussi redoutable que l'Allemagne...

Il a coûté à la France depuis 1870, en hommes et en argent, bien plus que la guerre actuelle.

L'Alcool flatte le palais; mais, véritable poison, il détruit l'organisme.

Les buveurs vieillissent vite. Ils perdent la moitié de leur vie normale et sont la proie facile d'infirmités et de maladies multiples.

Les "PETITS VERRES" des parents se transforment en GRANDES TARES héréditaires chez les descendants. La France leur doit environ deux cent mille fous, le double de poitrinaires, sans compter des goutteux, des ramollis avant l'âge et la plupart des criminels.

L'alcoolisme diminue des deux tiers notre production nationale, augmente la cherté de la vie et la misère.

A l'instar du Kaiser criminel, l'alcoolisme décime et ruine la France, à la plus grande joie de l'Allemagne.

Mères, jeunes gens, jeunes filles, épouses, agissez contre l'alcoolisme en souvenir des blessés et des morts glorieux pour la Patrie.

Vous accomplirez ainsi une tâche grandiose, égalant celle de nos héroïques soldats.

l'ALARME, Siège Social : PARIS, 45, rue Jacob

Helft! Helft!

! Schande !

Die Schamlosigkeit der Verwendung schwarzer Truppen zu Treibjagden auf Deutsche, die unter französischem Zwang selbst in den kleinsten Städchen erfolgende Einrichtung öffentlicher Häuser für Schwarze durch deutsche Behörden, die bestialische Verge- waltigung und die scheußlichen Notzuchtsverbrechen begangen an deutschen Mädchen, Frauen und Greisinnen von 6 bis 73 Jahren, die tierische Unzucht an 7 bis 11jhr. Knaben durch schwarze Wüstlinge schreit zum Himmel.

Gebt uns die Adressen

Euerer Freunde, Bekannten, Verwandten in Amerika, Spanien, Holland, Schweden Norwegen, Dänemark und England, damit wir dorthin berichten können: was uns aus hunderten von Briefen Angehöriger, Aerzte, Anwälte, aus beschworenen eigenen Aussagen und in den kurzen (von Frankreich zensierten!) Todesanzeigen dieser bemit- leidenswerten Opfer einer französischen Schandpolitik entgegenjammert!

Die gesamte Auslandspropaganda des Deutschen Notbundes muß durch freiwillige Spenden bezahlt werden. Darum gebt schnell und reichlich!

Helft durch Geld und Mitarbeit!

Völlige Verzweiflung ist heute das Los der deutschen Frau des besetzten Gebietes, wenn es nicht gelingt, durch eine vieltausendfache Anlage das Ausland wachzurütteln gegen eine Gefahr, die jetzt schon die weiße Rasse der ganzen Welt bedroht!

Die schwarze Schmach, heute begangen an der deutschen Frau!

Deutscher Notbund
gegen die schwarze Schmach

Fernspr. 30901 **München / Klarstraße 11o** Fernspr. 30901

---

96 FRANCE c. 1916

Abel Faivre

Alcohol is an enemy as dangerous as Germany. Since 1870, in men and money, it has cost France much more than the present war. Alcohol flatters the palate; but, a poison, it destroys the living creature. Drinkers grow old quickly. They lose half of their normal life and are an easy prey to multiple maladies and infirmities. The 'little drops' of the parents are the 'tipples' of the descendants. They have cost France 200,000 idiots, double the number of consumptives, not to mention the gout sufferers, the early-senile and the majority of criminals. Alcoholism divides our national production by two and increases misery — and the cost of living. Following the lead of the criminal Kaiser, drinking decimates and ruins France — to the great pleasure of Germany. Mothers, young men and women, wives, husbands! In memory of the glorious dead and wounded of our country, agitate against alcoholism. You will be doing a glorious task, equal to that of our heroic soldiers.

97 GERMANY 1919

Anonymous

SHAME! The shameless use of black troops to hunt down Germans; the establishment by German authorities, under compulsion by the French, of brothels for blacks even in the smallest towns; the bestial violation and rape of German women, young and old, between the ages of 6 and 75, the bestial perversions committed on 7- to 11-year old boys by black sex maniacs are crimes which cry to heaven. SEND US THE ADDRESSES of your friends, acquaintances and relatives in America, Spain, Holland, Sweden, Norway, Denmark and England to enable us to acquaint them with the deeds told in hundreds of letters from relatives, doctors and lawyers, in victims' sworn statements and in the brief death-notices of these tragic victims! The foreign propaganda of the Deutsche Notbund (German Emergency Federation) has to be met by voluntary contributions. Send your money quickly — and be generous! Let us have both money and cooperation! Utter desperation will befall the German women in the occupied areas unless we succeed in shaking up the other nations by accusing a thousandfold and warning against a danger which already threatens the white race all over the world! Today, German women are subjected to black ignominy! German Emergency Federation — the answer to the black insult. Munich/ Klarstrasse 11/o Telephone: 30901

POBLACHT NA H EIREANN.

THE PROVISIONAL GOVERNMENT
OF THE
IRISH REPUBLIC
TO THE PEOPLE OF IRELAND.

IRISHMEN AND IRISHWOMEN : In the name of God and of the dead generations from which she receives her old tradition of nationhood, Ireland, through us, summons her children to her flag and strikes for her freedom.

Having organised and trained her manhood through her secret revolutionary organisation, the Irish Republican Brotherhood, and through her open military organisations, the Irish Volunteers and the Irish Citizen Army, having patiently perfected her discipline, having resolutely waited for the right moment to reveal itself, she now seizes that moment, and, supported by her exiled children in America and by gallant allies in Europe, but relying in the first on her own strength, she strikes in full confidence of victory.

We declare the right of the people of Ireland to the ownership of Ireland, and to the unfettered control of Irish destinies, to be sovereign and indefeasible. The long usurpation of that right by a foreign people and government has not extinguished the right, nor can it ever be extinguished except by the destruction of the Irish people. In every generation the Irish people have asserted their right to national freedom and sovereignty; six times during the past three hundred years they have asserted it in arms. Standing on that fundamental right and again asserting it in arms in the face of the world, we hereby proclaim the Irish Republic as a Sovereign Independent State, and we pledge our lives and the lives of our comrades-in-arms to the cause of its freedom, of its welfare, and of its exaltation among the nations.

The Irish Republic is entitled to, and hereby claims, the allegiance of every Irishman and Irishwoman. The Republic guarantees religious and civil liberty, equal rights and equal opportunities to all its citizens, and declares its resolve to pursue the happiness and prosperity of the whole nation and of all its parts, cherishing all the children of the nation equally, and oblivious of the differences carefully fostered by an alien government, which have divided a minority from the majority in the past.

Until our arms have brought the opportune moment for the establishment of a permanent National Government, representative of the whole people of Ireland and elected by the suffrages of all her men and women, the Provisional Government, hereby constituted, will administer the civil and military affairs of the Republic in trust for the people.

We place the cause of the Irish Republic under the protection of the Most High God, Whose blessing we invoke upon our arms, and we pray that no one who serves that cause will dishonour it by cowardice, inhumanity, or rapine. In this supreme hour the Irish nation must, by its valour and discipline and by the readiness of its children to sacrifice themselves for the common good, prove itself worthy of the august destiny to which it is called.

Signed on Behalf of the Provisional Government,

THOMAS J. CLARKE.

SEAN Mac DIARMADA,	THOMAS MacDONAGH,
P. H. PEARSE,	EAMONN CEANNT,
JAMES CONNOLLY.	JOSEPH PLUNKETT.

The Provisional Government
... TO THE ...
CITIZENS OF DUBLIN

The Provisional Government of the Irish Republic salutes the CITIZENS OF DUBLIN on the momentous occasion of the proclamation of a

Sovereign Independent Irish State

now in course of being established by Irishmen in Arms.

The Republican forces hold the lines taken up at Twelve noon on Easter Monday, and nowhere, despite fierce and almost continuous attacks of the British troops, have the lines been broken through. The country is rising in answer to Dublin's call, and the final achievement of Ireland's freedom is now, with God's help, only a matter of days. The valour, self-sacrifice, and discipline of Irish men and women are about to win for our country a glorious place among the nations.

Ireland's honour has already been redeemed ; it remains to vindicate her wisdom and her self-control.

All citizens of Dublin who believe in the right of their Country to be free will give their allegiance and their loyal help to the Irish Republic. There is work for everyone : for the men in the fighting line, and for the women in the provision of food and first aid. Every Irishman and Irishwoman worthy of the name will come forward to help their common country in this her supreme hour.

Able-bodied Citizens can help by building barricades in the streets to oppose the advance of the British troops. The British troops have been firing on our women and on our Red Cross. On the other hand, Irish Regiments in the British Army have refused to act against their fellow countrymen.

The Provisional Government hopes that its supporters— which means the vast bulk of the people of Dublin—will preserve order and self-restraint. Such looting as has already occurred has been done by hangers-on of the British Army. Ireland must keep her new honour unsmirched.

We have lived to see an Irish Republic proclaimed. May we live to establish it firmly, and may our children and our children's children enjoy the happiness and prosperity which freedom will bring.

Signed on behalf of the Provisional Government,

P. H. PEARSE,
Commanding in Chief the Forces of the Irish Republic, and President of the Provisional Government.

Тов. Ленин ОЧИЩАЕТ землю от нечисти.

101 RUSSIA 1920

Deni (?)

*Comrade Lenin cleans the
world of garbage*

102 CHINA c. 1968

Anonymous
*Aim straight, hit hard, in
our determined struggle*

104 RUSSIA 1930

D.S. Moor
*Proletarians, be on your
guard! The 'Black Crows' [priests] are
preparing an attack on the USSR*

103 GERMANY 1919

Walter Ditz
*Heroes from the Front,
the homeland greets you*

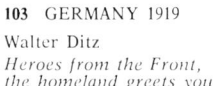

TALK WITH US

UNDERSTANDING IS FREE
UNDERSTAND US.
WE ARE PART OF ONE ANOTHER.
NO MORE THEM AGAINST US.
EACH ONE IS INDISPENSIBLE.
TALKING AND WORKING TOGETHER
WE CREATE AN EDUCATION.
EDUCATION MEANS
A LIFETIME GROWING WISER
IS THERE ANYTHING MORE IMPORTANT?
ALIVE WITH FEELING.
WISDOM EQUALS THOUGHT.
WHAT ELSE CAN ANSWER OUR QUESTIONS?
THE QUIET NOISE OF WISDOM WORKING.

THAT IS THE REVOLUTION

ISSUED BY THE ASSOCIATION OF MEMBERS OF HORNSEY COLLEGE OF ART

107 GERMANY 1923

Anonymous
*No, I will not
be intimidated!*

109 (UPPER SILESIA) 1921

Ant. Rom
*Be free from your oppressors.
Speak for Poland*

110 (UPPER SILESIA) 1921

Anonymous
*Don't be enslaved
by the corpse of Germany*

111 (UPPER SILESIA) 1921

St. L.
*Only the most stupid of calves
choose their own butcher*

112 GERMANY 1932
'Mjölnir' (Hans Schweitzer)
Our last hope: HITLER

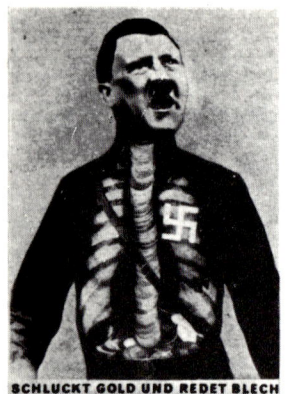

113 GERMANY 1930
John Heartfield
Gobbles gold, spews junk

SCHLUCKT GOLD UND REDET BLECH

115 GERMANY c. 1932
Anonymous
The Third Reich? NO!

114 BELGIUM c. 1939
Anonymous
That, NEVER!

ÇA JAMAIS!

116 POLAND 1952
Tadeusz Trepkowski
NO!

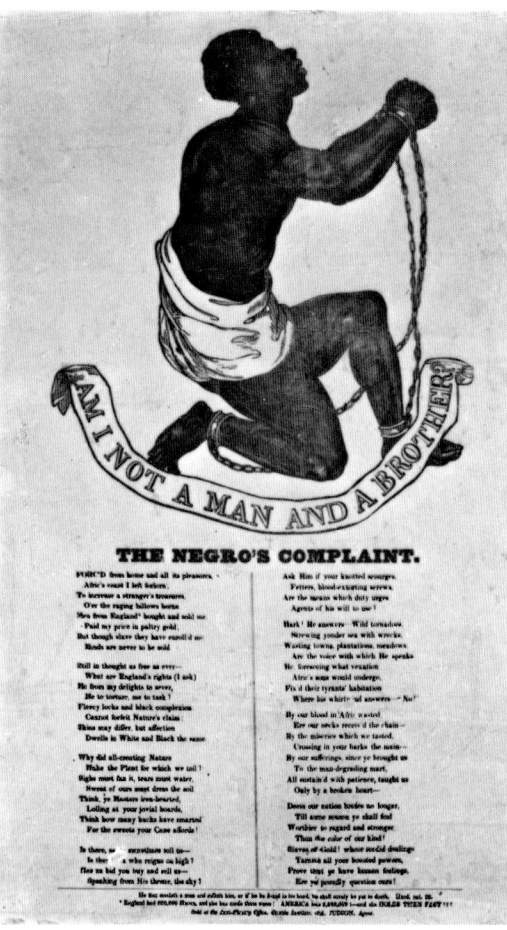

117 USA c. 1835
Anonymous

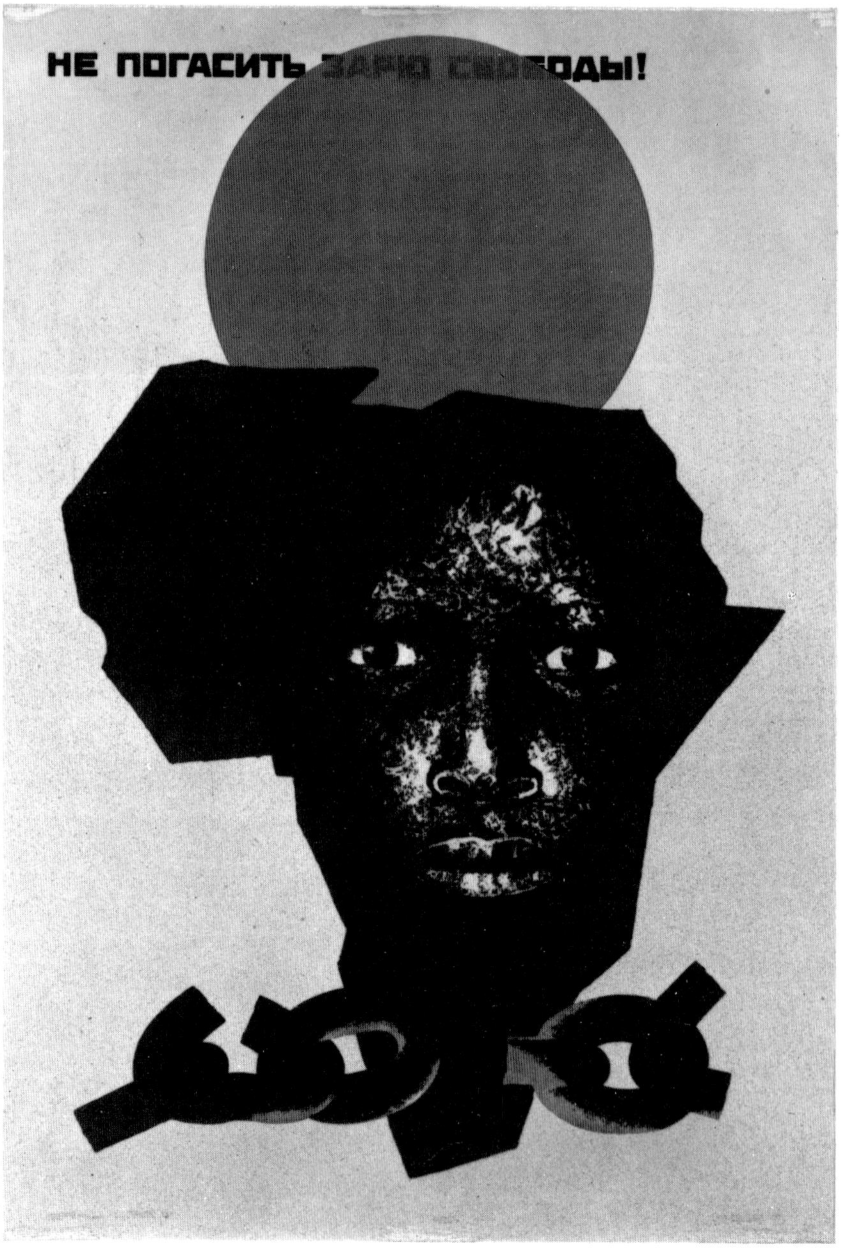

119 RUSSIA 1967
V. Karakashev
Let not the dawn of freedom fail

CAUTION!!
COLORED PEOPLE
OF BOSTON, ONE & ALL,

You are hereby respectfully CAUTIONED and advised, to avoid conversing with the

Watchmen and Police Officers
of Boston,

For since the recent ORDER OF THE MAYOR & ALDERMEN, they are empowered to act as

KIDNAPPERS
AND
Slave Catchers,

And they have already been actually employed in KIDNAPPING, CATCHING, AND KEEPING SLAVES. Therefore, if you value your LIBERTY, and the Welfare of the Fugitives among you, Shun them in every possible manner, as so many HOUNDS on the track of the most unfortunate of your race.

Keep a Sharp Look Out for
KIDNAPPERS, and have
TOP EYE open.

APRIL 24, 1851.

118 USA 1851
Anonymous

SLAVERY
still exists!

● It exists in 30 countries of the 'free' world

● In one country alone 1,000,000 live as serfs

● In another country one harem contains 300 women

● Children are still being sold into drudgery

● The UN Convention on Slavery is openly flouted

The ANTI-SLAVERY
SOCIETY
still exists!

Started in 1823, the Society's continued existence is a reminder of a task unfinished. Please help us to end slavery once and for all. For free information write to the Chairman, Sir Douglas Glover TD,MP Anti-Slavery Society, Denison House, 296 Vauxhall Bridge Road, London, SW1   Telephone: 01-834 6065

121 BRITAIN 1970
Anonymous

JORNADA DE SOLIDARIDAD CON EL CONGO/13 DE FEBRERO·DAY OF SOLIDARITY WITH THE CONGO/FEBRUARY 13·JOURNÉE DE SOLIDARITE AVEC LE CONGO/13 FEVRIER

120 CUBA 1968
Anonymous
Day of Solidarity with the Congo, Feb. 13

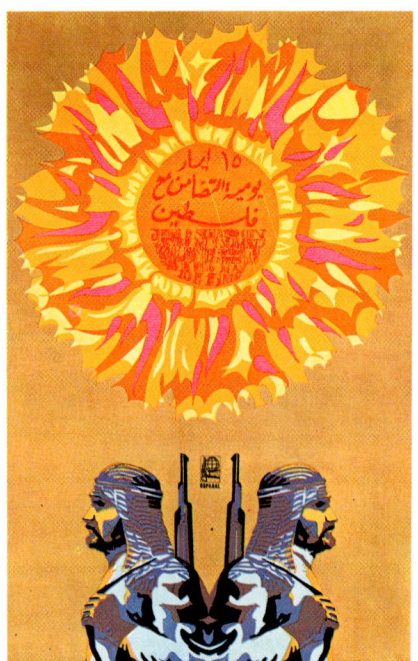

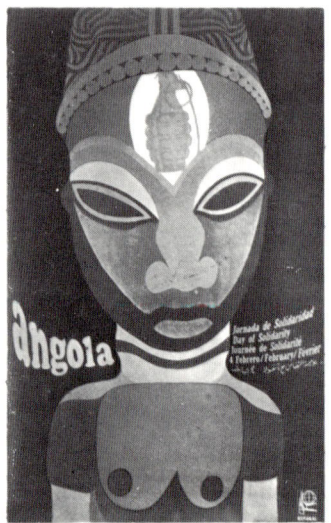

122 CUBA 1968
Anonymous
Day of Solidarity with Palestine, May 15

123 CUBA 1968
Anonymous
International Week of Solidarity with Latin America, April 19-25

124 CUBA 1968
Anonymous
Angola: Day of Solidarity, February 4

angola
Jornada de Solidaridad
Day of Solidarity
Journée de Solidarité
4 Febrero/February/Février

125 CUBA 1968
Anonymous

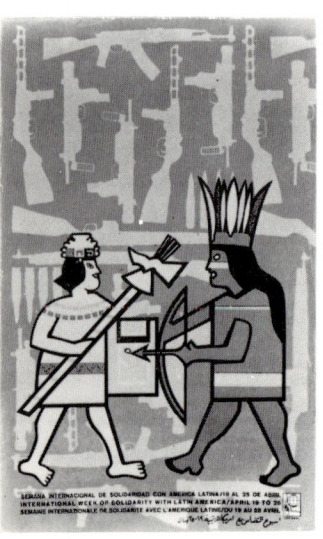

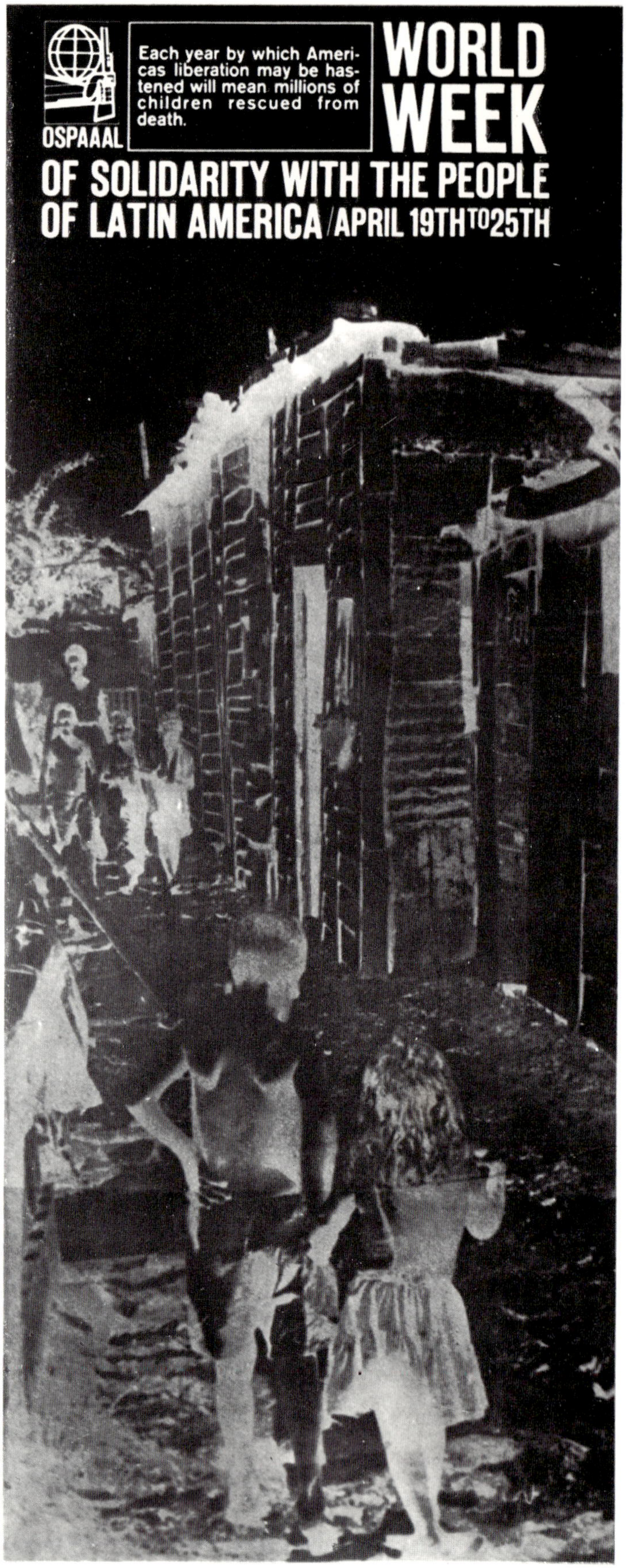
OSPAAAL
Each year by which Americas liberation may be hastened will mean millions of children rescued from death.
WORLD WEEK
OF SOLIDARITY WITH THE PEOPLE OF LATIN AMERICA/APRIL 19TH TO 25TH

DIA DEL GUERRILLERO HEROICO 8 DE OCTUBRE
JOURNEE DU GUERILLERO HEROIQUE 8 OCTOBRE
DAY OF THE HEROIC GUERRILLA OCTOBER 8

يوم المغاور الباسل ٨ تشرين اول

126 CUBA 1968
Anonymous

GOD, OUR COUNTRY AND LIBERTY.!!

127 USA 1861
Anonymous

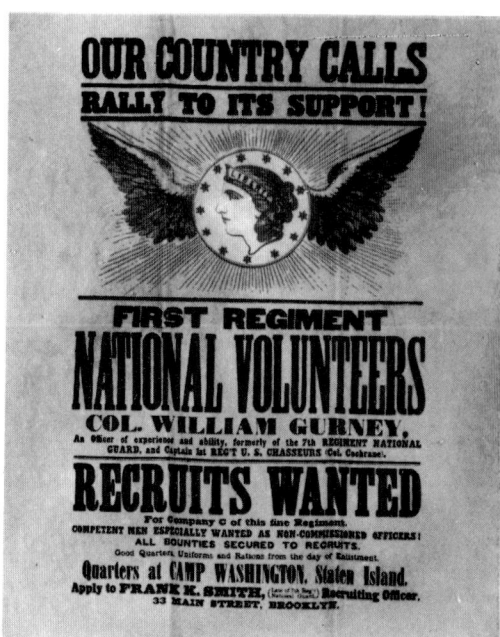

OUR COUNTRY CALLS
RALLY TO ITS SUPPORT!

FIRST REGIMENT
NATIONAL VOLUNTEERS
COL. WILLIAM GURNEY.

An Officer of experience and ability, formerly of the 7th REGIMENT NATIONAL
GUARD, and Captain 1st REG'T U. S. CHASSEURS Col. Cochrane.

RECRUITS WANTED

For Company C of this fine Regiment.
COMPETENT MEN ESPECIALLY WANTED AS NON-COMMISSIONED OFFICERS!
ALL BOUNTIES SECURED TO RECRUITS.
Good Quarters, Uniforms and Rations from the day of Enlistment.

Quarters at CAMP WASHINGTON, Staten Island.
Apply to FRANK K. SMITH, Recruiting Officer.
33 MAIN STREET, BROOKLYN.

128 USA 1861
Anonymous

130 USA (Confed.) 1862
Anonymous

MULLIGAN'S
BRIGADE!
LAST CHANCE TO AVOID THE DRAFT!
$402 BOUNTY!
TO VETERANS!
$302 to all other VOLUNTEERS!

All Able-bodied Men, between the ages of 18 and 45 Years,
who have heretofore served not less than nine months, who shall reenlist for Regiments
in the field, will be deemed Veterans, and will receive one month's pay in advance,
and a bounty and premium of $402. To all other recruits, one month's pay in advance,
and a bounty and premium of $302 will be paid.
All who wish to join Mulligan's Irish Brigade, now in the field, and to receive the
magnificent bounties offered by the Government, can have the opportunity by calling
at the headquarters of

CAPT. J. J. FITZGERALD

Of the Irish Brigade. Otis Rountree, United States Mustering Recruiting Officer, Chicago Illinois.

Each Recruit, Veteran or otherwise, will receive

Seventy-five Dollars Before Leaving General Rendezvous,
and the remainder of the bounty in regular instalments till all is paid. The pay,
bounty and premium for three years will average **$24** per month for Veterans,
and **$21.30** per month for all others.

If the Government shall not require their whole charge for the full period of Three Years and they shall be mustered before
out of the service before the expiration of their term of enlistment, they shall receive, UPON BEING MUSTERED OUT,
the whole amount of BOUNTY remaining unpaid, the same as if the full term
been served.

Chicago December 1863

J. J. FITZGERALD,
Recruiting Officer, over a North Clark & Lake Streets

129 USA 1863
Anonymous

BUTLER'S PROCLAMATION

An outrageous insult to the Women of New Orleans.

Southern Men, avenge their wrongs!!!

Head-Quarters, Department of the Gulf,
New Orleans, May 15, 1862.

General Orders, No. 28.

As the Officers and Soldiers of the United States
have been subject to repeated insults from the women calling themselves ladies of New Orleans, in
return for the most scrupulous non-interference
and courtesy on our part, it is ordered that here-
after when any Female shall, by word, gesture, or
movement, insult or show contempt for any officer
or soldier of the United States, she shall be regard-
ed and held liable to be treated as a woman of the
town plying her avocation.

By command of Maj.-Gen. BUTLER,
GEORGE C. STRONG,
A. A. G. Chief of Stables.

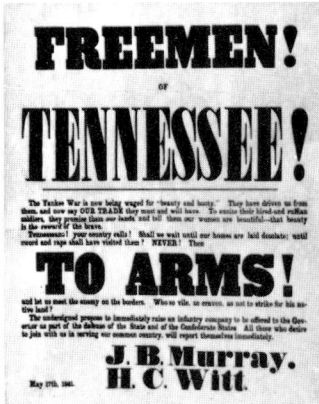

FREEMEN!
of
TENNESSEE!

The Yankee War is now being waged for "booty and beauty." They have driven us from them, and now say OUR TRADE they must and will have. To entice their kind and ruffian soldiers, they promise them our lands and tell them our women are beautiful—that booty is the reward of the brave.

Tennesseans! your country calls! Shall we wait until our houses are laid desolate, until sword and rape shall have visited them? NEVER! Then

TO ARMS!

and let us meet the enemy on the borders. Who so vile, so craven, as not to strike for his native land?

The undersigned propose to immediately raise an infantry company to be offered to the Governor as part of the defense of the State and of the Confederate States. All those who desire to join with us in serving our common country, will report themselves immediately.

J. B. Murray.
H. C. Witt.

May 17th, 1861.

131 USA (Confed.) 1861

Anonymous

Head Quarters, Virginia Forces,
STAUNTON, VA.

MEN OF VIRGINIA, TO THE RESCUE!

Your soil has been invaded by your Abolition foes, and we call upon you to rally at once, and drive them back. We want Volunteers to march immediately to Grafton and report for duty. Come one! Come ALL! and render the service due to your State and Country. Fly to arms, and succour your brave brothers who are now in the field.

[Done by Authority.]
M. G. HARMAN, Maj. Commd'g
at Staunton.
J. M. HECK, Lt. Col. Va. Vol.
R. E. COWAN, Maj. Va. Vol.
May 30, 1861.

132 USA (Confed.) 1861

Anonymous

THE ENEMY
IS APPROACHING!

DEFENCE of the STATE!
AND HAVE Called THE MILITIA for that PURPOSE!
A. G. CURTIN, Governor of Pennsylvania.

APPLY AT
FALSTAFF HOTEL, N.W. cor. 6th & Jayne
Capt. JOHN McCORMACK.
J. CARTER, 1st Lieut.

133 USA 1863

Anonymous

---

134 USA 1865

Anonymous

SURRENDER OF GEN. LEE!

"The Year of Jubilee has come! Let all the People Rejoice!"

200 GUNS WILL BE FIRED
On the Campus Martius,
AT 3 O'CLOCK TO-DAY, APRIL 10,
To Celebrate the Victories of our Armies.

Every Man, Woman and Child is hereby ordered to be on hand prepared to Sing and Rejoice. The crowd are expected to join in singing Patriotic Songs.

ALL PLACES OF BUSINESS MUST BE CLOSED AT 2 O'CLOCK.

Hurrah for Grant and his noble Army.

By Order of the People.

135 USA 1969

Ronald and Karen Bowen
(The design is based on Rosenthal's
famous picture of the raising
of the American flag on Mount
Suribachi on Iwo Jima, 1945.)

136 HOLLAND 1969

Hans Buter

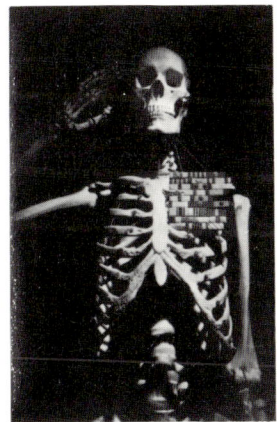

137 USA 1969

Stewart and Corby

138 JAPAN 1969

Hirokatsu Hijikata

139 BRITAIN 1906

Anonymous

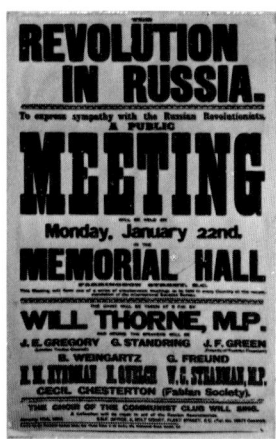

140 RUSSIA 1968

C. Datskevitch and
A. Lemeschenko

The country's winged defence — famed for flying high

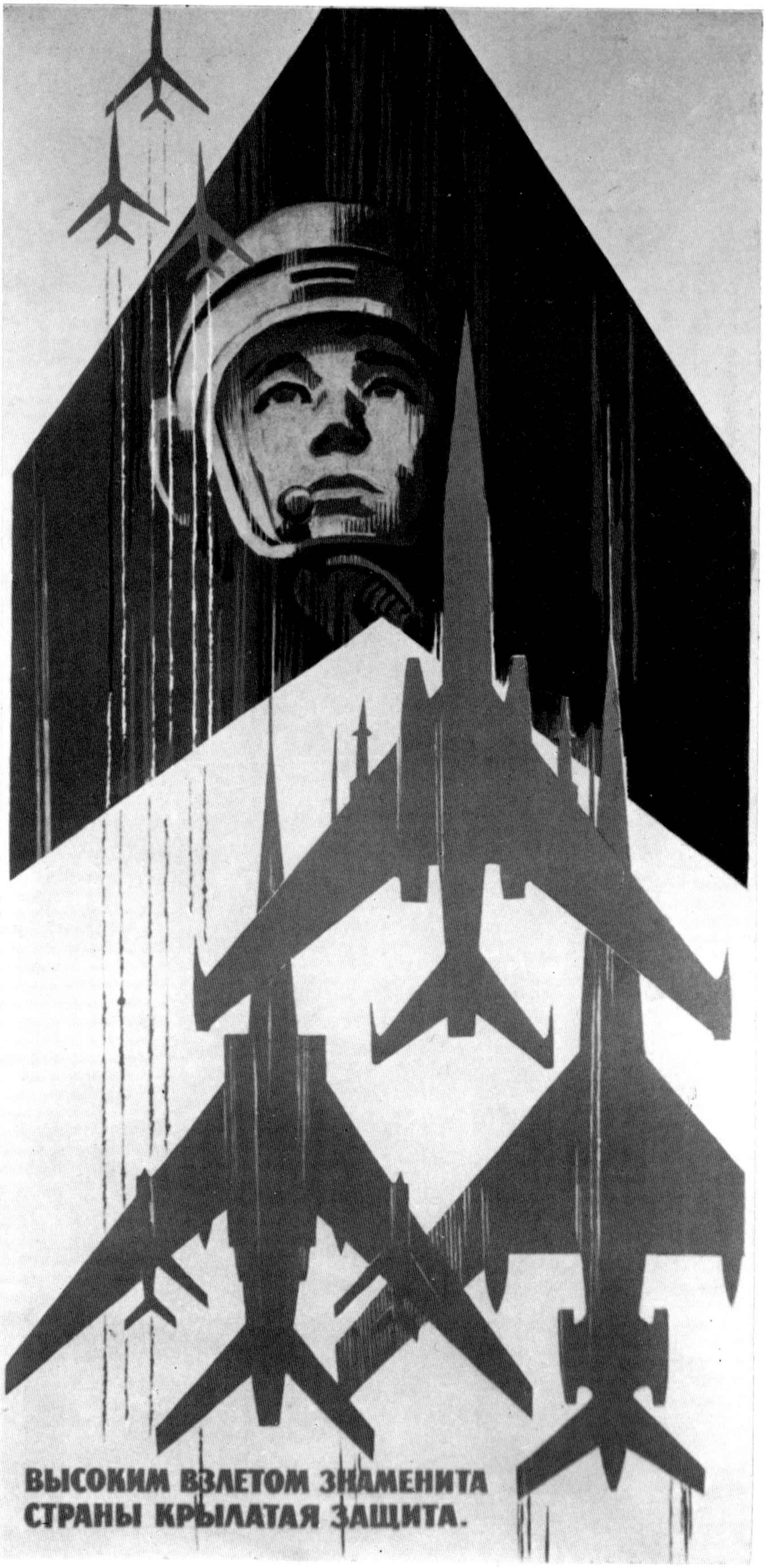

141 RUSSIA 1917

Anonymous

Notice: By the Officer Commanding the Petrograd District. In recent days disorders have occurred in Petrograd; these were accompanied by attacks and threats on the lives of military and police personnel. All gatherings in the streets are hereby prohibited. I hereby warn the people of Petrograd that the Military have been given my instructions to use their weapons and to take all measures necessary to restore order in the capital.

— Lt. Gen. Khabalov Feb. 25 1917.

ОБЪЯВЛЕНІЕ

Командующаго войсками Петроградскаго военнаго Округа.

Последніе дни въ Петроградѣ произошли безпорядки, сопровождавшіеся насиліями и посягательствами на жизнь воинскихъ и полицейскихъ чиновъ.

Воспрещаю всякое скопленіе на улицахъ.

Предваряю населеніе Петрограда, что мною подтверждено войскамъ употреблять въ дѣло оружіе, не останавливаясь ни передъ чѣмъ для водворенія порядка въ столицѣ.

Командующій войсками Петроградскаго военнаго Округа,
Генералъ-Лейтенантъ Хабаловъ.

25-го февраля 1917 года.

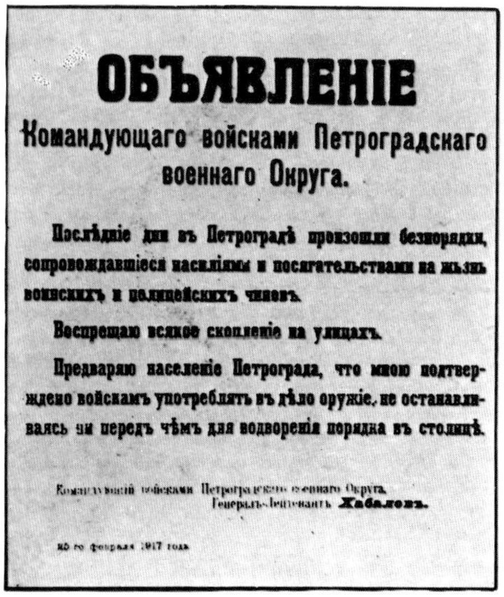

Приказъ № 1.

1 марта 1917 года.

По гарнизону Петроградскаго Округа всѣмъ солдатамъ гвардіи, арміи, артиллеріи и флота для немедленнаго и точнаго исполненія, а рабочимъ Петрограда для свѣдѣнія.

Совѣтъ Рабочихъ и Солдатскихъ Депутатовъ постановилъ:

1) Во всѣхъ ротахъ, батальонахъ, полкахъ, паркахъ, батареяхъ, эскадронахъ и отдѣльныхъ службахъ разнаго рода военныхъ управленій и на судахъ военнаго флота немедленно выбрать комитеты изъ выборныхъ представителей отъ нижнихъ чиновъ вышеуказанныхъ воинскихъ частей.

2) Во всѣхъ воинскихъ частяхъ, которыя еще не выбрали своихъ представителей въ Совѣтъ Рабочихъ Депутатовъ, избрать по одному представителю отъ ротъ, которымъ и явиться съ письменными удостовѣреніями въ зданіе Государственной Думы къ 10 часамъ утра, 2-го сего марта.

3) Во всѣхъ своихъ политическихъ выступленіяхъ воинская часть подчиняется Совѣту Рабочихъ и Солдатскихъ Депутатовъ и своимъ комитетамъ.

4) Приказы военной комиссіи Государственной Думы слѣдуетъ исполнять только въ тѣхъ случаяхъ, когда они не противорѣчатъ приказамъ и постановленіямъ Совѣта Рабочихъ и Солдат. Депутатовъ.

5) Всякаго рода оружіе, какъ то винтовки, пулеметы, брониро-ванные автомобили и прочее должны находиться въ распоряженіи и подъ контролемъ ротныхъ и батальонныхъ комитетовъ и ни въ коемъ случаѣ не выдаваться офицерамъ даже по ихъ требованію.

6) Въ строю и при отправленіи служебныхъ обязанностей сол-даты должны соблюдать строжайшую воинскую дисциплину, но внѣ службы и строя, въ своей политической, общегражданской и частной жизни солдаты ни въ чемъ не могутъ быть умалены въ тѣхъ правахъ, коими пользуются всѣ граждане.

Въ частности, вставаніе во фронтъ и обязательное отданіе чести внѣ службы отмѣняется.

7) Равнымъ образомъ отмѣняется титулованіе офицеровъ: ваше превосходительство, благородіе и т. п., и замѣняется обращеніемъ: господинъ генералъ, господинъ полковникъ и т. д.

Грубое обращеніе съ солдатами всякихъ воинскихъ чиновъ и, въ частности, обращеніе къ нимъ на «ты», воспрещается и о всякомъ на-рушеніи сего, равно какъ и о всѣхъ недоразумѣніяхъ между офице-рами и солдатами, послѣдніе обязаны доводить до свѣдѣнія ротныхъ комитетовъ.

Настоящій приказъ прочесть во всѣхъ ротахъ, батальонахъ, полкахъ, экипажахъ, батареяхъ и прочихъ строевыхъ и нестроевыхъ командахъ.

Петроградскій Совѣтъ Рабочихъ и Солдатскихъ Депутатовъ.

142 RUSSIA 1917

Anonymous

Order I: March I, 1917. To all soldiers of the Guard, the Army, the Artillery and the Fleet, of the Garrison of Petrograd and to the workers for their information: The Soviet of Workers and Military Deputies decrees;
1: The electing of committees of representatives of Other Ranks of all Companies, Battalions, Regiments, Depots, Batteries and Squadrons, and all individual service units of the Military Command on vessels of the navy.
2: At all military units which have not elected their re-presentatives to the Soviet of Workers Deputies, one representative to be elected forthwith in each.
3: In all their political activities the Military will be governed by the Soviet of Workers and Soldiers Deputies and their committees.
4: Orders issued by the Military Commissioner of the State Duma are to be executed only when they do not conflict with orders and decrees of the Soviet of Workers and Soldiers Deputies.
5: All weapons, including rifles, machine guns, armoured cars etc. must be at the ready and under the control of the Company and Battalion Committees. In no case must they be placed at the disposal of officers, even if demanded.
6: When in formation for carrying out service duties, soldiers must observe strictest military discipline, but when not on service duties or in formation, soldiers may not in any way be deprived of the rights of ordinary citizens in their political, public and personal lives. In particular, standing to attention and obligatory saluting when not on duty are abolished.
7: Equally, the addressing of officers as 'Your Excellency, Your Highness' etc. is abolished and replaced by the following form of address; Mr General; Mr Colonel. Rudeness to soldiers of any military units, and in parti-cular the use of the familiar 'thou' is forbidden and all cases of infringement must be reported by the soldiers to their Company Committee.
This order is to be read in all Companies, Battalions, Regiments, to all crews and batteries and other units and non-military personnel.
— *Soviet of Workers & Soldiers Deputies*

143 RUSSIA 1968

E. Aprunian

For the international solidarity
of the working class

V. Koretski

Our forces are numberless

НАШИ СИЛЫ
НЕИСЧИСЛИМЫ
В. Корецкий

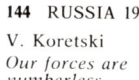

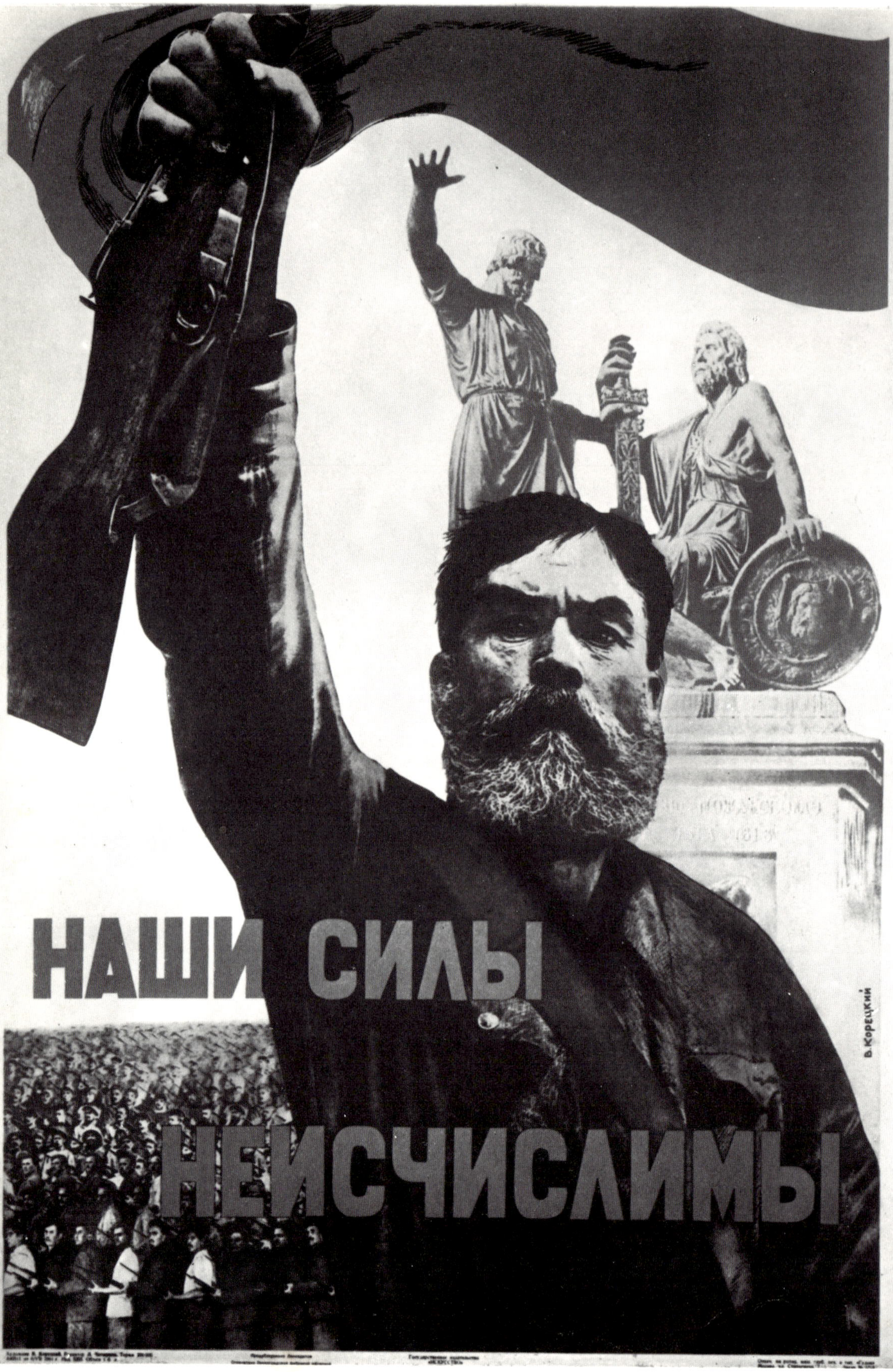

坚决支持香港爱国同胞
的正义斗争！

145 CHINA 1968
Anonymous
Support our patriotic
Hong Kong
brethren
in their just
and rightful struggle

ALLA GIOVENTÙ

La guerra ingrossa; i pericoli aumentano. La Patria ha bisogno di voi.

Chi v' indirizza queste parole ha combattuto, per onorare come meglio poteva, il nome Italiano in lidi lontani; è accorso, con un pugno di valenti compagni, da Montevideo per aiutare anch' egli la vittoria patria o morire su terra Italiana.

Egli ha fede in voi; volete, o giovani, averla in lui?

Accorrete: concentratevi intorno a me: l' Italia ha bisogno di dieci, di venti mila volontari; raccoglietevi da tutte le parti in quanti più siete; e alle Alpi! Mostriamo all' Italia, all' Europa, che *vogliamo* vincere e vinceremo.

Milano, 27 luglio 1848.

G. GARIBALDI.   383891

Tipografia Eredi Rezzoni.

146   ITALY 1848

Anonymous

TO YOUTH
The war spreads; dangers increase. The country has need of you. He who addresses these words to you has fought, as best he could, in order to do honour to the name of Italy in distant shores. He has hastened home with a handful of gallant comrades, from Montevideo, himself to help the victorious country - or to die on Italian soil.
He has faith in you. Will you not return that faith?
Make haste! Gather round me! Italy needs ten, twenty thousand volunteers. Come from everywhere, no matter where you are - to the Alps! Let us show Italy - and Europe - that we have the will to win. And we will win.

148   BRITAIN 1942
S. John Woods

147   RUSSIA 1920

D. S. Moor
Cossack: whose side are you on?
Theirs or ours?

坚决反击
英帝国主义!
毛泽东选集
祖国千百万红卫兵坚决支持港九爱国同胞反英抗暴斗争!

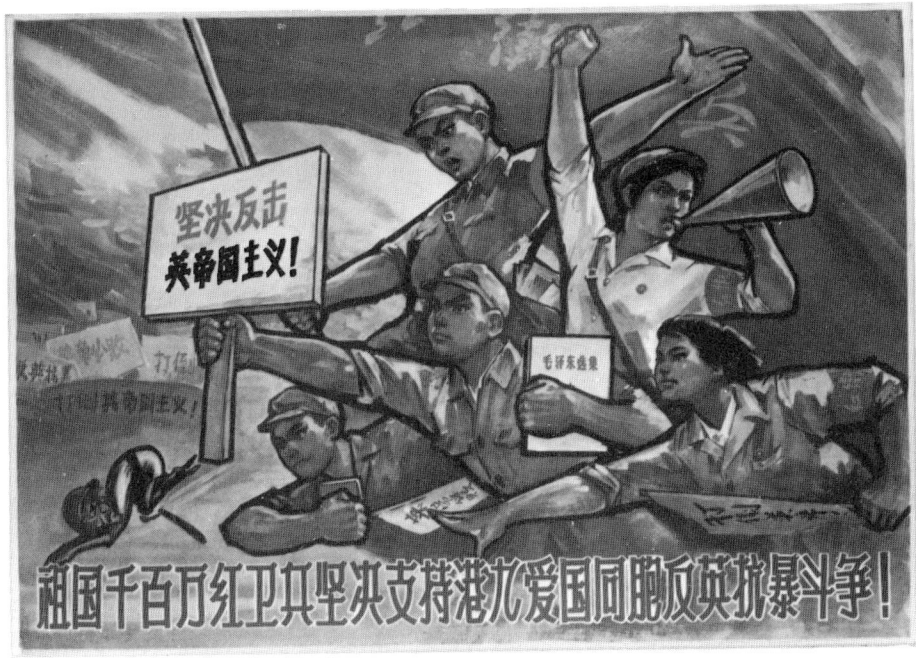

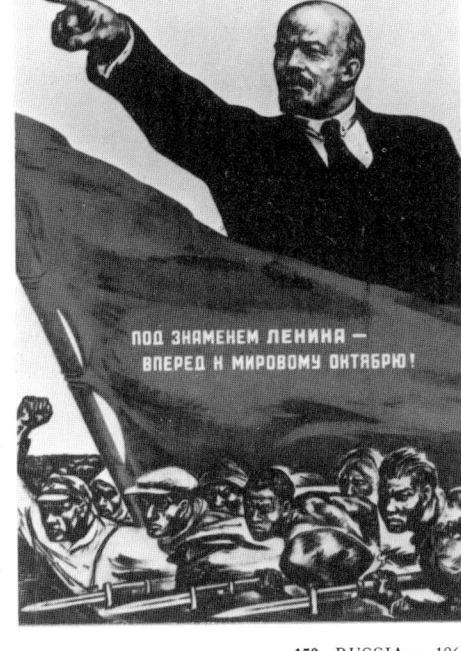

149 CHINA c. 1968

Anonymous

Tens of millions of Red Guards of the Fatherland are solidly behind the nine Hong Kong patriots in their struggle against British Imperial tyranny

ПОД ЗНАМЕНЕМ ЛЕНИНА —
ВПЕРЕД К МИРОВОМУ ОКТЯБРЮ!

150 RUSSIA c. 1965

(.....?)

Under the flag of Lenin – forward to world revolution

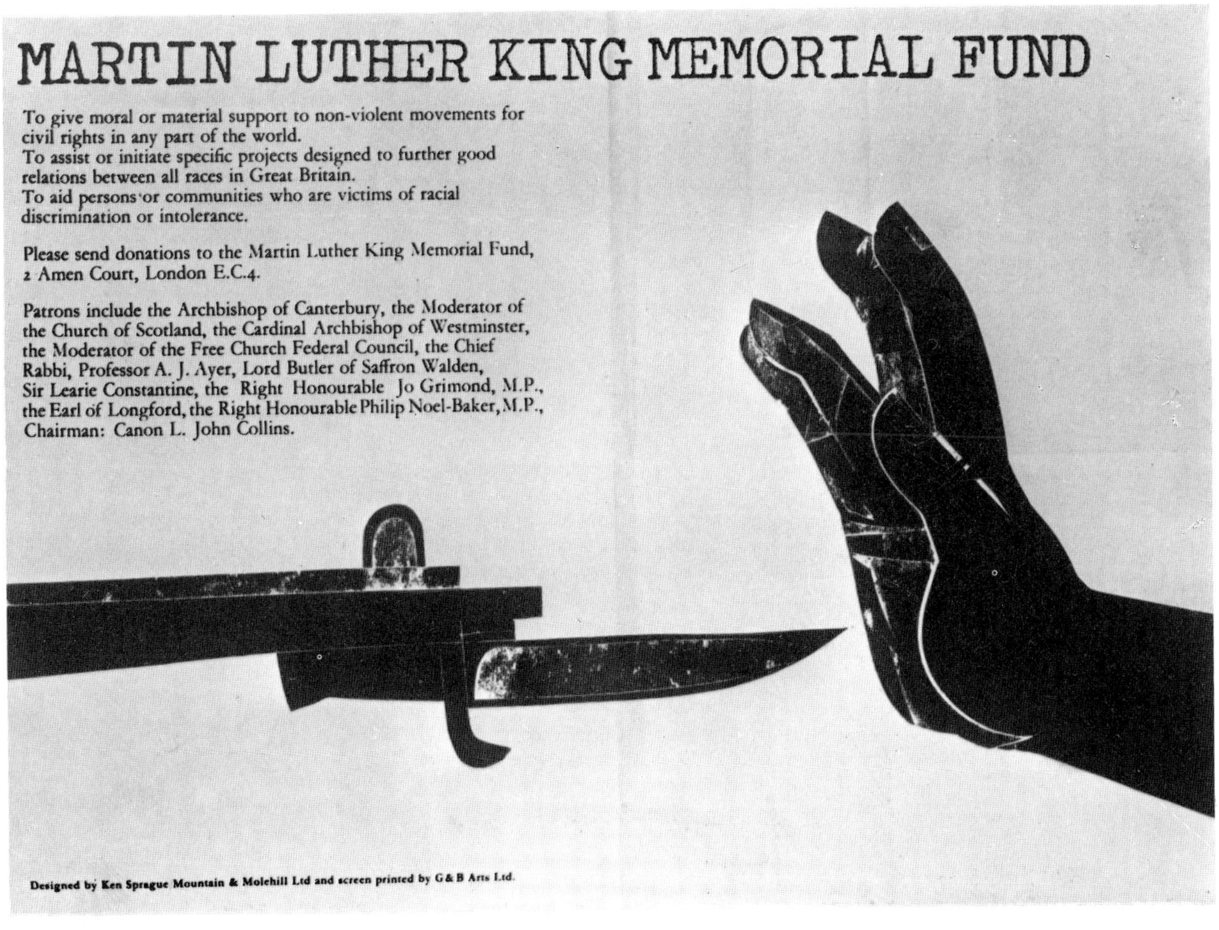
MARTIN LUTHER KING MEMORIAL FUND
To give moral or material support to non-violent movements for civil rights in any part of the world.
To assist or initiate specific projects designed to further good relations between all races in Great Britain.
To aid persons or communities who are victims of racial discrimination or intolerance.
Please send donations to the Martin Luther King Memorial Fund, 2 Amen Court, London E.C.4.
Patrons include the Archbishop of Canterbury, the Moderator of the Church of Scotland, the Cardinal Archbishop of Westminster, the Moderator of the Free Church Federal Council, the Chief Rabbi, Professor A. J. Ayer, Lord Butler of Saffron Walden, Sir Learie Constantine, the Right Honourable Jo Grimond, M.P., the Earl of Longford, the Right Honourable Philip Noel-Baker, M.P., Chairman: Canon L. John Collins.
Designed by Ken Sprague Mountain & Molehill Ltd and screen printed by G & B Arts Ltd.

151 BRITAIN 1968

Ken Sprague

153 BRITAIN 1968
Seabrook/Graves

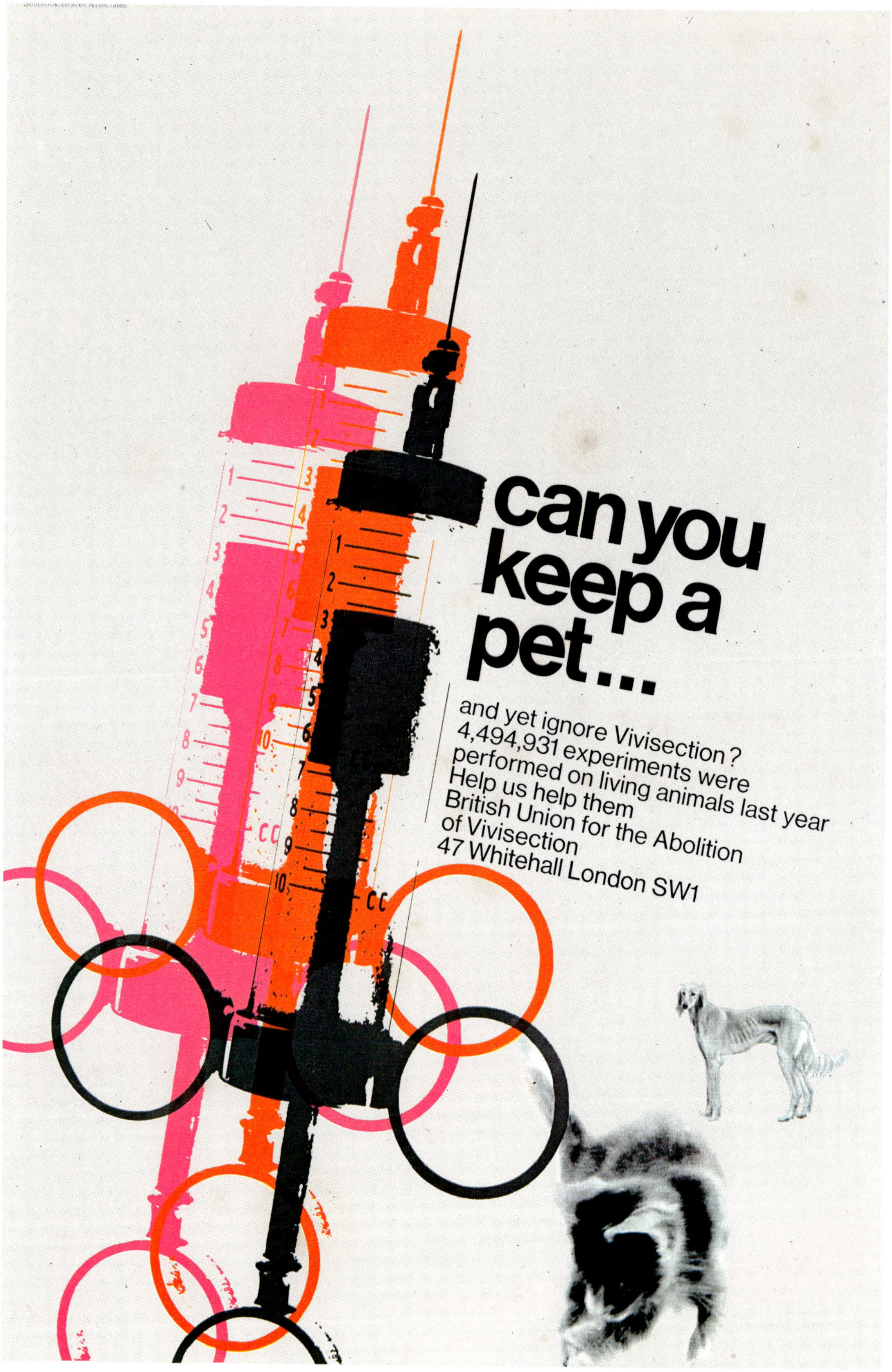
can you keep a pet...
and yet ignore Vivisection?
4,494,931 experiments were performed on living animals last year
Help us help them
British Union for the Abolition of Vivisection
47 Whitehall London SW1

152 BRITAIN 1968
Anonymous

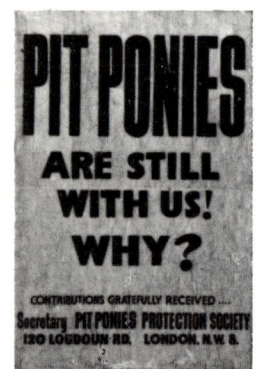

PIT PONIES
ARE STILL WITH US!
WHY?
CONTRIBUTIONS GRATEFULLY RECEIVED ...
Secretary PIT PONIES PROTECTION SOCIETY
120 LOUDOUN RD. LONDON, N.W. 8.

158 BRITAIN 1958
Anonymous

159 BRITAIN 1958
M and M

LIVERPOOL STEALS WELSH WATER

160   BRITAIN 1965
Anonymous

STOP ROBBING WALES

161   BRITAIN 1965
Anonymous

WELSH WATER IS PART OF OUR HERITAGE WE WILL DEFEND IT

162   BRITAIN 1965
Anonymous

LIVERPOOL - HANDS OFF WALES

163   BRITAIN 1965
Anonymous

164   BRITAIN 1969
Anonymous
Wales (ticked); *Britain* (crossed out)

Arwr, Sant.

CARLO

Y Lolfa

165   BRITAIN 1969
(.....?)
Hero, Saint Charles
(Carlo is a name commonly given
in Wales to a dog)

VIVA ESPAÑA

CVARTEL GENERAL DEL GENERALÍSIMO

PARTE OFICIAL DE GVERRA, CORRESPONDIENTE AL DIA DE HOY

EN EL DÍA DE HOY, CAVTIVO Y DESARMADO EL EJÉRCITO
ROJO, HAN ALCANZADO LAS TROPAS NACIONALES SVS
VLTIMOS OBJETIVOS MILITARES

LA GVERRA HÀ TERMINADO

BVRGOS, 1 DE ABRIL DE 1939 .. AÑO DE LA VICTORIA ..

El Generalísimo,

166   SPAIN 1939

Anonymous
*General Headquarters of the Generalissimo. Official War Communiqué
for today April 1 1939, Year of the Victory. Today, with the Red Army captive
and disarmed, the National troops have achieved their final
military objectives. The war has ended.
— El Generalissimo: Franco*

AVVISO

Bergamo, li 8 Giugno 1859.

Si ordina a tutti i pubblici funzio-
narj di rimanere ai loro posti e di
attendere senza ritardo al disimpegno
delle loro mansioni, salvo quelle parti-
colari disposizioni che il Governo
credesse di prendere.

IL REGIO COMMISSARIO STRAORDINARIO PRESSO IL
GENERALE GARIBALDI
EMILIO VISCONTI VENOSTA.

167   ITALY 1859

Anonymous
*Notice: All public officials
are ordered to remain at their
posts and to proceed without
delay upon the discharge
of their duties, except for any
special instructions the
Government may give.
On behalf of
General Garibaldi
— Emilio Visconti Venosta*

169   BRITAIN c. 1965

Ken Sprague

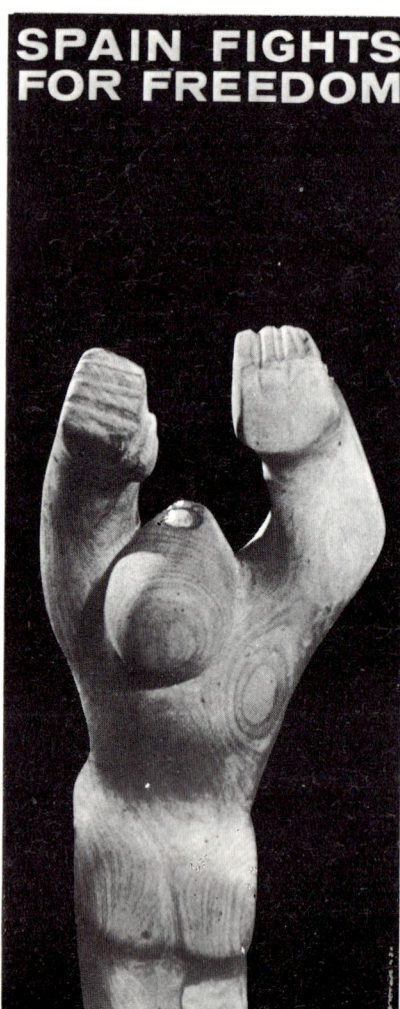

SPAIN FIGHTS
FOR FREEDOM

DÉCRET

Le **PRINCE NAPOLEON** au nom du **PEUPLE FRANÇAIS** décrète ce
qui suit:
La Dynastie des Bourbons d'Orléans a cessé de régner.
Le Peuple Français est rentré dans ses droits.
Les Troupes sont déliées du serment de Fidélité.
La Chambre des Pairs et la Chambre des Députés sont dissoutes. Un con-
grès national sera convoqué dès l'arrivée du Prince Napoléon à Paris.
Monsieur Thiers Président du Conseil est nommé à Paris Président du Gou-
vernement Provisoire.
Le Maréchal Clausel est nommé Commandant en chef des Troupes rassemblées
à Paris.
Le Général Pajol conserve le commandement de la première Division Militaire
Tous les Chefs de corps qui ne se conformeront pas sur le champ à ces or-
dres seront remplacés.
Tous les Officiers, sous-Officiers et Soldats qui montreront énergiquement
leur sympathie pour la cause nationale, seront récompensés d'une manière é-
clatante au nom de la Patrie.
Dieu protège la France!

signé: **NAPOLÉON**

Boulogne le   **1840**

168   FRANCE 1840

Anonymous
*Decree: The Prince
Napoleon, in the
name of the French
people, decrees as
follows: The dynasty
of the Bourbons
d'Orleans has ceased
to reign; the French
people are reinstated
in their rights;
the troops are
absolved from their
oaths of allegiance;
both Chambers are
dissolved. A National
Congress will be
called on the arrival
of Prince Napoleon
in Paris...
Commanders who fail
to conform
immediately to these
orders are hereby
replaced; all officers,
non-commissioned
officers and other
ranks who show
their keen sympathy
for the national
cause will be notably
rewarded in the name
of the Country.
May God protect
France.
— Napoleon*

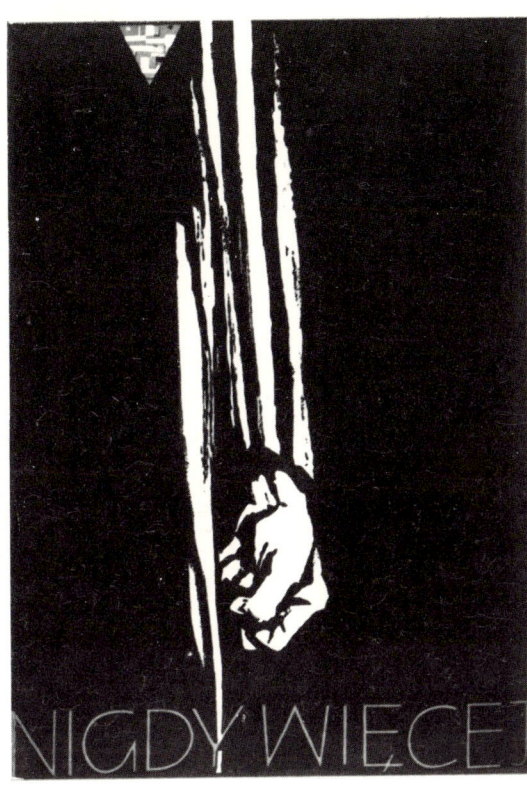

NIGDY WIĘCEJ

170 POLAND 1955

Zbigniew Kaja
Never again!
(The striped overall
was the uniform of
inmates of German
concentration camps)

171/2 FRANCE c. 1942

Anonymous
*If you want France to live, you will fight
in the Waffen SS against Bolshevism.*
(In the second picture the caption
has been amended by partial obliteration.
It reads: *If you want France to live,
you will fight against the Boche.*)

173 GERMANY c. 1944

Anonymous
*'Died on the last day
of the Second World War'.
Do you want to be
the last to die?* (Illegal poster)

174 GERMANY 1944

Anonymous
A sixth winter of war?
(Illegal poster)

175 BRITAIN c. 1950

Walter E. Spradbery

THE BUILDING OF A
PEACEFUL
FUTURE
IS
THREATENED
BY
GERMANY
RE-ARMING

176 BRITAIN 1968

Anonymous

GREECE?
Tourist - better wait
to next year
MIGHT BE SAFER

177 BRITAIN c. 1960

Anonymous

boycott
apartheid
DON'T BUY SOUTH AFRICAN GOODS

178 GERMANY c. 1968

Anonymous
*Workers and students against
the Emergency Powers Act*

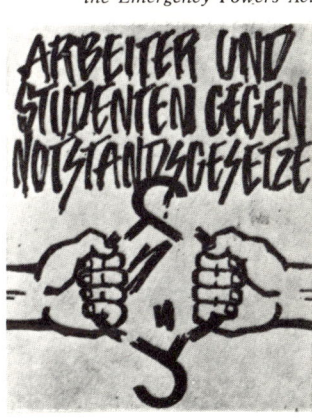

ARBEITER UND
STUDENTEN GEGEN
NOTSTANDSGESETZE

179 ITALY 1943

Anonymous
Committee of National Liberation of the City of Milan: Milanese!
From today — by order of the National Committee of Liberation for Upper Italy —
the final phase of the national insurrection goes into effect. Workers in the factories,
patriots of the Liberty Volunteer Corps in the streets are struggling to liberate Milan
from the fascist rabble. Mussolini, torn between fear and the exercise of his
customary deceit, has attempted his last contortions: he has asked for surrender —
and then absented himself from its signing. The call for the surrender of the residue
of the fascists, who, conscious of the accumulation of crimes to which it has to
answer, still resist in the city, must be firm and inexorable. The Committee of National
Liberation calls the people to the final struggle. The Allies must find the city cleared
of fascists, confident in itself, single-mindedly confronting the future.
Milanese!
April 26 will be a glorious date in the history of our city. Follow the instructions
that the Committee has given you in its first manifesto; join the patriots in the
battle; give shelter to the wounded; reward the fighters with the unanimity of your
endeavour, with the dignity of your bearing, and the brotherly solidarity of free men.
For the fascists, one choice: Surrender or perish.
— *Committee of National Liberation, City of Milan*

COMITATO LIBERAZIONE NAZIONALE
DELLA CITTA' DI MILANO

MILANESI!

Da ieri · con l'ordine del COMITATO DI LIBERAZIONE NAZIONALE PER
L'ALTA ITALIA · la fase culminante dell'insurrezione nazionale è in atto.

Gli operai nelle fabbriche, i patrioti del CORPO VOLONTARI DELLA LIBERTÀ
nelle strade si battono per liberare Milano dalla canaglia fascista.

Mussolini, incerto tra la paura e l'inveterata abitudine all'inganno, ha tentato
le sue ultime contorsioni, chiedendo la resa e sottraendosi, poi, alla firma della
capitolazione.

La intimazione di resa contro i residui della sbirraglia fascista che, cosciente
del cumulo di delitti di cui deve rispondere, ancora resiste in città, deve essere
ferma e inesorabile.

IL COMITATO DI LIBERAZIONE NAZIONALE chiama il popolo alla lotta finale.

Le truppe alleate devono trovare la città ripulita dai fascisti, fidente in se
stessa, concorde nella ripresa, protesa verso il suo avvenire.

MILANESI!

Il 26 aprile sarà una data gloriosa nella storia della nostra città.

Seguite le istruzioni che il Comitato vi ha impartito nel suo primo manifesto,
unitevi ai patrioti nella battaglia, ospitate i feriti, premiate i combattenti con la
concordia della vostra opera, la dignità del vostro contegno e la solidarietà fraterna
che vi consacra uomini liberi.

Per i fascisti una sola alternativa:

ARRENDERSI O PERIRE

Da Palazzo Marie · 26 Aprile 1945

IL COMITATO DI LIBERAZIONE NAZIONALE
DELLA CITTA' DI MILANO

MOVIMENTO SOCIALE ITALIANO

La situazione che a Milano, come in tante altre
città d'Italia, si è determinata a causa delle agitazioni
strumentalizzate dal marxismo e supinamente subite
dal Governo, ha esasperato la generalità dei cittadini.

Molte delle contestazioni che giovani e lavoratori
fanno sono giustificate: il sistema contro il quale si
elevano le proteste è proprio quello che soltanto il Movimento Sociale Italiano, unica forza di vera ed effetti-
va opposizione, combatte strenuamente da oltre un ven-
tennio.

Il Movimento Sociale Italiano non accetta e non
può approvare, però, che le opposizioni al sistema si
manifestino colpendo moralmente e materialmente le
Forze dell'Ordine e le Forze Armate, ingiuriando e per-
cuotendo le persone ed arrecando danni ai cittadini.

La Federazione Milanese del Movimento Sociale
Italiano non vuole prendere, in questo momento, ini-
ziative e ciò per evitare speculazioni, ma si rivolge ancora una volta, ai combattenti di tutte le guerre, ai giovani, ai cittadini che hanno sentimento nazionale, ai lavoratori liberi da ipoteche politiche perchè affermino la
volontà che sia restaurata l'autorità dello Stato, di uno
Stato, però ristrutturato nel suo sistema e nel quale le
forze del lavoro, della produzione e i giovani abbiano
potere decidente.

Milano, dicembre 1968

Il Commissario
della Federazione del M.S.I.
On. Avv. NICOLA ROMEO

181 GREECE c. 1942

Anonymous
National Liberation Front;
Unity – the Nation's
Guiding Light

182 GREECE c. 1942

Anonymous
National Unity; All to the War!

180 ITALY 1969

Anonymous
Italian Social Movement.
The situation which has, in Milan as in other cities, been brought about through agitation engineered by Marxism, and weakly submitted to by the Government, has exasperated the majority of citizens.
Many of the complaints made by workers and young people are justified; the system against which protests are made is precisely that which only the Italian Social Movement, alone as a true and effective voice of opposition, has struggled strenuously against for over twenty years.
The Italian Social Movement does not accept and cannot approve opposition to the system which, both morally and materially damages the Forces of Order and the Armed Forces, injuring persons and occasioning harm to citizens.
The Milanese Federation of the Italian Social Movement does not seek at this moment to take action, but it calls again to ex-soldiers, to young people and to all citizens who are free from political bias, that they may affirm their will for the restoration of the authority of the State - a state, however, which is re-structured in its system, and in which both labour and youth play a decisive role.
- Nicola Romeo
Milan Federation of the Italian Social Movement
Milan, December 1968

185 GREECE 1969

Anonymous
Freedom for Political Prisoners!

186 GREECE 1969

Anonymous
No!

184 ITALY 1969

Anonymous
We will free our comrades from the bosses' prisons

183 GREECE 1969

Anonymous

187 FRANCE 1968

Anonymous
(ORTF: Organisation of French
Radio and Television)

189 ITALY 1969

'GAL'

The Voice of the Bosses; God gave it to me; woe to him who touches it!
(The secret thought of the Christian Democrats)

188 FRANCE 1968

Anonymous
(Design reversed in error; corrected design appears on right)

PAS DE RECTANGLE BLANC POUR UN PEUPLE ADULTE:

INDÉPENDANCE et AUTONOMIE de l'O.R.T.F.

190 FRANCE 1968 Anonymous
No white patch for an adult people: Independence and autonomy for ORTF
(The white patch is used to censor children's TV programmes)

191 FRANCE 1968
Anonymous
His Master's Voice

192 FRANCE 1968
Anonymous
ORTF in combat

193 ITALY 1969 'GAL'
You pay: fight
for a liberated TV service

194 FRANCE 1968
Anonymous
Poison comes into the home

195 FRANCE 1968
Anonymous
To give in a little
is to give up altogether

196 ITALY 1969
Anonymous
No to piece-work; No to injuries

197 ITALY 1969
'GAL'
(The Bosses' Press)
The Industrial Armchair

198 FRANCE 1968
Anonymous
At Citroën the workers
will sweep away
traitors and cowards

199 BRITAIN 1968
Anonymous

200 RUSSIA c. 1921
Krinski

201 ITALY 1969
Anonymous
Youth, fight blasphemy and obscenity!

202 FRANCE 1968
Anonymous
All together comrades, till victory

203 ITALY 1969
Anonymous
*40,000 workers in the struggle
— only a beginning*

204 FRANCE 1968
Anonymous
*Impetus is given for
a long struggle*

TELL JOHNSON STOP THE BOMBING

205 BRITAIN 1968

Ken Sprague

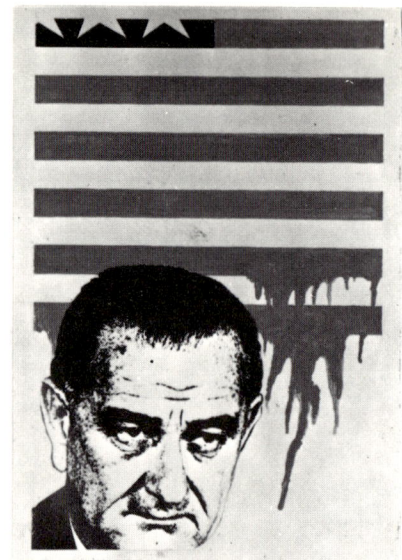

206 BRITAIN 1968

Ken Sprague

VIET NAM

MR JOHNSON TE LO AVEVAMO DETTO...

207 ITALY 1969

Anonymous

Vietnam: Johnson, we told you ...

ĐỘC LẬP THỐNG NHẤT HÒA BÌNH

208 SOUTH VIETNAM 196

Le Toan

For independence, reunification and peace

VIETNAM SUMMER 1967

129 MT. AUBURN STREET · CAMBRIDGE, MASSACHUSETTS 02138 · TELEPHONE (617) 492-6700

209 USA 1967
Anonymous

210 HOLLAND 1969
Anonymous
Protest against higher burdens on motor traffic

211 AMERICA 1968
Gary Brown

214 BRITAIN 1967

215 AMERICA 1968
Tomi Ungerer

212 USA 1968
Anonymous

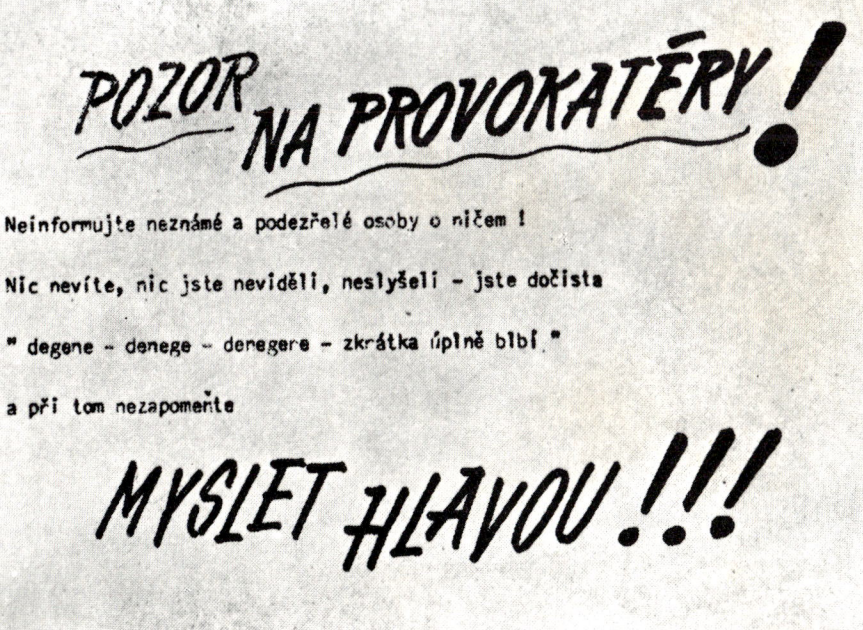

213 USA (?) 1889
Anonymous

216 CZECHOSLOVAKIA 1968
Anonymous
Beware agents-provocateurs. Give no information to strangers.
Stammer and stutter and look degenerate. In short, behave completely
daft. But don't forget, use your head!

217 SWEDEN 1969
Anonymous
Boycott the Athens European Games

218 USA 1968
Anonymous

219 BRITAIN c. 1928
Anonymous

U.S.A. SURPASSES ALL THE GENOCIDE RECORDS!

KUBLAI KHAN MASSACRES 10% IN NEAR EAST

SPAIN MASSACRES 10% OF AMERICAN INDIANS

JOSEPH STALIN MASSACRES 5% OF RUSSIANS

NAZIS MASSACRE 5% OF OCCUPIED EUROPEANS AND 75% OF EUROPEAN JEWS

U.S.A. MASSACRES 6.5% OF SOUTH VIETNAMESE & 75% OF AMERICAN INDIANS

FOR CALCULATIONS & REFERENCES WRITE TO: P.O.BOX 180, NEW YORK, N.Y. 10013

221 USA 1968
Anonymous

220 USA 1968
Pinkerton

222 BRITAIN 1967
Anonymous

224 USA 1969
Anonymous

223 USA 1968
Ben Shahn

225 ITALY 1969 Anonymous
NATO costs us 4,000 million lire a day.
Spend for peace, not for war

226 BRITAIN c. 1935
Anonymous

227 BRITAIN 1964
Anonymous

228 BRITAIN 1969
Anonymous

POSTERS
with information to
undermine all that
other information -
all that $ $ $ $.
resistance work···
join the poster
workshop - artists!
hands!   money!
people & cheques to
the poster workshop